BUILDING A LEGACY

THE BILL PULTE STORY

ISBN: 0-917939-12-3

Printed in Canada
10 9 8 7 6 5 4 3 2 1

Publisher: Pulte Homes, Inc.
Executive Editor: David McNally
Writer: Joe Schuler
Design & Production: SangFroid Press

BUILDING A LEGACY

THE BILL PULTE STORY

Table of Contents

Dedication

This is the book Bill Pulte wouldn't want us to write.

Why not? In all that Bill stands for – doing for others, never self-serving – the concept of a lifetime tribute, a book, instinctively couldn't be accepted by Bill's humble nature.

This ordinary man has put a remarkable stamp on this company and its people, and even, on this country and world of ours. He is a true American entrepreneur. Yet, we're certain some businessmen even in his hometown of Detroit don't know the name of Bill Pulte, chairman of a 56-year-old company with thousands of shareholders. A company that builds hundreds of houses a day – one of the nation's largest homebuilders.

But we know a deeper part of Bill. He would trust us, he would trust us *as he always has*, his friends and his employees, his Pulte Homes family, to share the deeply layered mosaic of his life, and the vivid testimony it presents us, *as a light to our future*. We offer it not as a biography, but as a sketch, a portrait, a tool to reveal an ordinary man, who, by example, lives an extraordinary life.

We have a vibrant future ahead if we embody the virtues and principles of a man named Bill. His hands shaped our future, like the hands of the turn-of-the-century craftsmen who wore smooth the grips of the tools framed in our Michigan headquarters.

So, when Bill gets a chance to read this book and reflect on the foundation he laid for us, a foundation told here through reminiscences of family, friends, and colleagues past and present, we're confident he'll say: "I'm glad it's written down." Because it will become a blueprint of sorts for all who follow his vision.

"You follow me? You follow me?"

How many times has Bill asked us that? That's not a chairman in his seventies looking back, but someone whose eyes insistently look ahead, whose feet are moving fast, whose mind is moving still faster, and he's hoping all the while that we're right behind him.

What few people outside this organization know is that in true Pulte style, with little fanfare, Bill Pulte has built a legacy here. A legacy to the spirit of American entrepreneurship and business that is so far-reaching we couldn't begin to paint a complete picture of its 56-year expanse, even in a book.

We'd like every member of the Pulte Homes family to consider this collection of biographical essays a tribute and guide for us all, so that together we can treasure and carry on what we've been given. Bill's gentle leadership, his reassurance, his vision, his love, and his laughter, live in our 50 divisions and rest in the heart of each of the more than 400,000 homes we've built.

Sometimes you have to leaf through old photo albums not only to relive the past, but also to gain a sense for the future. Bill, however, never lives in the past. But, through his stories, he loves to take people back and give the historical perspective: *"This is how it got to where it is."*

So, slip back in time. Experience colorful pieces of Bill's story, laugh with him, and see how we arrived where we are: A $14 billion public company with more than 13,000 of us working with the power of one man's vision. Through this story, see where we're headed.

You are a wonderful light, Bill Pulte. From all of us at Pulte Homes, thank you. We *will* follow.

And, like you, *we will lead.*

February 8, 2006

"The greatest measure of one's success is inner peace."
— Bill Pulte

Introduction

"Hi, my name is Bill!"

So real, *so human*. People who meet Bill Pulte use those words to describe him, after looking him in the eye and sensing his easy-going manner.

Shake his hand, and you'd never know he chairs a company that provides a living to thousands of people, who work together building homes in neighborhoods all across America.

His colorful sweaters and grandfatherly ways give no indication that this man heads one of the largest companies in the country. A firm that started with a suggestion from his own grandmother back in 1948: *"Billy, you're pretty good with your hands. Why don't you get a job as a carpenter?"*

Bill's not a man to relive former glories, or bathe in success. He knows through achievement, through common-sense thinking, he has made his future, and that of thousands of others, even brighter.

Bill builds to fulfill happiness. Not just his own but that of others – especially others. While corporate America has grown fond of saying "customers first," Bill has always put employees first, knowing that if his employees were happy, his customers would be too.

Bill Pulte's contribution to the Fortune 500 is that he's running a modern business by age-old values. He leads in an industry that always has had a lock on the heart of America. It is a trust Bill embraces with his own heart.

This is an American story. Bill Pulte has lived from the rise of production automobiles to the dawn of production housing. He has seen tradesmen become entrepreneurial businessmen, then national builders. He has led that evolution. He has lived through housing recessions, rust belt recessions, double-digit interest rates, and fundamental changes in American housing needs, from the bungalow to the split level to the so-called smart houses of today.

He has propelled the integration of America through the birth of the suburb. He has contributed to the creation and design of planned communities. Through his innovations, he helped shape the American home. Long a student of auto manufacturing, he is helping to shape the precise, factory-made home of tomorrow.

All the facets of Bill's personality may never be revealed, but to illuminate parts of who he is and what he has accomplished, we present these essays to honor Bill: the Family Man, the Entrepreneur, the Competitor, the Whiz Kid, the Teacher, the Leader, the Quiet Giver, the Visionary.

Values, Clear & Simple

You can clearly see what is important to Bill by visiting his third-floor office in our Bloomfield Hills headquarters. Behind Bill's desk, to the east, you see an expansive modern painting by West Virginia artist Lawrence Roy. It stretches the length of the wall and only Bill and the artist know its meaning, but in its essence, it implies *color and motion*. Movement is progress for Bill Pulte. Color is happiness. He lives in motion and reclines in color – his orange leather desk chair attests to that.

Next to the desk sits a hardwood toolbox, that of an 18th century trades-man, and to the south beyond, a half-wall of glass. To the west, straight ahead, more glass, where, from the desk, you see no ground, *only trees and blue sky.*

It is an appropriate sight line … from the toolbox, to the windswept treetops, where Bill's vision of what's next is out there, waiting to be created. What will change, what will be made better, faster, and more efficient?

Current reality is right beneath the windows, on the floor, on the couch, in stacks of paperwork and building materials – casing, shingle, siding samples – that signify the chairman's initiatives – fine-tuning the supply chain, or examining options that will make building homes simpler, yet *always, always* better.

To the right is his modest drafting room, a closet at best, where he scans floor plans, or examines factory production systems before heading down to the first floor to chat with architects or executives in Pulte Home Sciences' offices.

Beside the drafting room, to the right of Bill's desk, the north, is where the deepest facet of Bill Pulte is cut.

A crucifix hangs on that wall. Given to him by Adam Cardinal Maida, Roman Catholic Archbishop of Detroit. It's a thank you for one of Bill's many quiet acts of kindness. On the cross is someone who dwells at the center of Bill's life, someone whose philosophy is his own – an insistent, gently delivered: *"Come, follow me."*

Bill Pulte is a man who has been nurtured by the love of his God, and whose goal is to do the same for others … always.

"The first thing in life has got to be your God. Second is your family. And, if we do things right here, your Pulte family's third."

This tribute is for a man whose vision is astonishing in its clarity and simplicity. A vision that unfolds in the most American of traditions, in the most American of cities. It is a vision made possible through compassion, loyalty, integrity, and determination.

It is a vision built with innovative thinking, an understanding of the craftsman and the customer, and the need to surround oneself with capable leaders, and business know-how.

But mostly, it's a vision inspired by a love for people.

All people.

This is Bill Pulte's story.

"I never went to work a day in my life.
I just loved what I was doing."

The two-year-old Bill Pulte.
"You follow me?"

© Joe Crachiola

Chapter One
The Family Man

Grow up in a family of eight, in the heart of the Great Depression. Provide for a family of 16 while yearning to become America's biggest, and best, home builder.

Grasp that, and you'll understand why Bill Pulte's story begins at home.

Appreciate that Bill's father, also William John, had to move his family five times from apartments or rental homes in Ann Arbor and Detroit before his eldest son, at 19, built a house for them. Then, you'll understand why home, and homes, are important to Bill Pulte.

Values a leader holds dear are often the ideals he embraced as a child. Having a home, for Bill, means having a cherished place to live. A place where memories begin. A place to learn. *A place to be yourself*. A place where stories, *where legacies*, can root.

Through his family – James T. Lynch, his grandfather, was a cement contractor – Bill learned to love the trade, love hard work, and love the rewards work enabled him to bring others.

He learned self confidence. Kindness. Toughness. *Persistence*.

As a teen, then as a father providing for his family, Bill developed the principles fundamental to Pulte Homes, and to his leadership: Take risks. Stay calm in chaos. Change to grow. Simplify the complex. *Always* use common-sense.

He'd learn *never* to sweat the small stuff, not to worry about the past, *always* to look to the future.

> "Pulte Homes started with a family attitude, and it has stayed that way. It seems harder sometimes, but it really isn't. You just make small families in each city."

He would learn that humility was the wellspring of virtue, and self-confidence. He'd learn how, through example, he could change the world. He'd learn, as later his children and company would learn, *there's no such thing as "can't."*

Bill would discover kitchens were places to exchange ideas – and build mountainous ice cream sundaes. He always knew that people were important, no matter their place in the pecking order, but came to learn that teams of people can accomplish much more.

He would begin to shape a way of thinking and business that would someday become *The Pulte Way.*

"You've got to remember," Bill says, *"that no matter what happens, the first thing in life has got to be your God. The second thing has got to be your family. And then, if we do things right here, your Pulte family's third."*

Those words define Bill Pulte's true gauge of success: *Inner peace.*

Optimism: 9 Cents

Three years after the 1929 stock market crash, when 5 million people out of work were lamenting in song, *Brother, Can You Spare a Dime?*, Marguerite Lynch Pulte gave birth to her first child, William John the 3rd. It was May 16, 1932.

Bill was born during a visit to his mother's parents in Detroit. The influences of the Motor City on Bill's thinking would reverberate through all his days. From the 1950s, when he dreamed of creating "the General Motors of Home Building;" to the 1980s when he began assembling prototypes in his garage and was learning how to produce houses as quickly as automobiles; or when he envisioned the housing market divided into consumer segments; to the 2000s, 70 years from his birth, when *Forbes* reported that his vision was now clearly becoming a reality. Auto manufacturing methods and philosophies would intrigue and influence Bill all his life.

The Great Depression also gave birth to another housing legend: The bungalow. Sears, Roebuck and Co., and Montgomery Ward shipped bungalow kits nationwide. The second home Bill built borrowed from this housing style. His early models provided solutions for families moving to the suburbs from these modest homes: The earliest move-up buyers.

But that's getting ahead of our story.

From Ann Arbor, Bill's dad, an automobile adjuster, visited wrecks in neighboring towns. With millions unemployed, he was lucky to have work, and he worked hard. He had to, because besides Bill, he also had to support daughter Maureen, and four more sons Pat, Mike, Bob, and Tim.

On the side, Bill's dad kept the grounds for a golf course and driving range, where Bill and his brothers later helped him retrieve golf balls from mosquito-swarmed ponds. Perhaps this was the genesis of one of Bill's great passions: The love of the lost golf ball.

"We were on the poor side growing up," says the chairman. He remembers Ann Arbor had no school bus. His parents didn't have the 9 cents for him and his school-age brother and sister to take the municipal bus each day. So unless driving rain or sleet prevented them, they walked two miles to school, and two miles back. "But in the spring and fall it was great," says Bill, "because we could ride our bikes."

And so, Bill's optimism was born.

"We were on the poor side growing up. My parents didn't even have the 9 cents for my sister and me to ride the bus to school."

A broadly smiling Bill (on the far left) expresses his natural optimism in this 1937 photo of his kindergarten class.

Life Keys: Faith & Friends

The Roman Catholic nuns at St. Thomas School taught Bill toughness.

"You had to be silent and walk in line, almost like the Army's boot camp," he recalls. "I broke the rules whenever I could … I didn't like walking in line." In third grade, he joined the Cub Scouts, and again was asked to march in line. "Two meetings of the Cub Scouts and I got out," Bill says.

But the young Pulte didn't need to march far to discover what it took to be a leader. His heroes were right at home. "My mother and father *were* my role models, no question about that," Bill says. "Probably one of the greatest things they taught me was self-confidence."

On the other hand, they also taught Bill not to be arrogant. "They didn't teach by sitting you down, they just lived it," he recalls. Integrity was another quality that was very important to the Pultes. Bill later told his children that his father had the most integrity of any man he'd known.

Once Bill had passed his teenage years, he began to realize that integrity defined a person's character more than anything else.

"My mother and father were my role models, no question about that... They taught me... self-confidence."

He participated in Mass each morning at St. Thomas, and he continues to live a life of devotion to this day. His faith's precepts, woven into the fabric of his life, give him a vital source of renewable optimism and energy. They continue to shape his priorities – he strives to live a life of charity, humility, restraint, fortitude, and love.

This devotion would be vital to a life-long pursuit of these virtues. Joe Baranska, Bill's high school buddy and first sales and marketing vice president, once observed: "I've often thought: If somebody has the self discipline to get up and go to church every morning, even when he's out of town, if nothing else, that gives you an hour of thinking. If nothing else … your mind is going to stay clear.

"And has that been the rudder in his life? Has that been the key?"

A Key, And A Door, Combined

Bill's Grandpa Lynch helped him open more doors to accomplishment and self-confidence. Beginning when Bill was about eight years old, during summer vacations, Bill began helping his grandfather, the contractor. When he was a teenager, this experience was enough to land him summer jobs working for an Italian immigrant home builder on Detroit's east side.

Being elected 7th grade class president continued to build his confidence as well as being one of the top five athletes (there were only 35 in the class, he modestly admits). "We played sandlot ball," he says. "There was no Little League."

When his father was promoted during Bill's freshman year of high school, the family moved to a house in Detroit, their fifth house during Bill's childhood. Despite the string of relocations, it was the first change that affected him. But as Bill began to learn and would someday teach, all change carries an upside.

At his new high school, De La Salle, run by the Christian Brothers, he made lifelong friends. "My best friend turned out to be the first new guy I met at De La Salle," Bill says. That same friend, Fred Rozelle, golfed with him before their high school reunion, 55 years later.

Bill (second from left) and friends at prayer.

The top-five athlete in 7th grade.

Seeing Orange

Another friend eventually became Bill's first full-time employee – Dave Kellett. Dave says Bill didn't always seem to project purpose. At least one teacher worried about his lack of industriousness. Bill and Brother Brendan had their differences. Brother Brendan warned Bill he would become a ditch-digging failure, if he didn't mend his ways. Dave says the teacher once clunked Bill on the head with a weighty copy of *Prose and Poetry*, shouting: "Billy, get some life into you!"

A loyal Irishman, Brother Brendan was particular about St. Patrick's Day. On one St. Patrick's Day, Bill left home, his coat buttoned to the neck. He didn't shed the jacket until he reached Brother Brendan's class. And then, there he was: Wearing a bright *orange* sweater.

This was no accident – it was Bill's wonderful sense of humor. As Bill learned in history class, orange is the color of Northern Irish Protestants. King William of Orange defeated King James II, a Roman Catholic, in 1690. Northern Ireland Protestants are called the Orangemen; green stands for the Irish Catholic nationalists of the south, and revolution.

There was no revolution at De La Salle that day. But the Irish Brother ordered Bill out of the room. When the principal ran into the young "orange man" in the hallway, he enjoyed the joke and led Bill back to class. This prank became a legend as it was retold on the radio every St. Patrick's Day by another De La Salle graduate, Detroit radio personality J.P. McCarthy.

It was the first of many colorful Bill Pulte stories to come. From his orange desk chair he now leads a public corporation where the green of earnings comfortably blends with the intangible glow of family values.

Between De La Salle's Christian Brothers and his disciplinarian dad, Bill learned valuable benefits of self-control. "I think that's part of where he got his toughness," his sister Maureen says.

When he wasn't pulling pranks, Bill and his brother Pat pulled oars on the rowing team. Bill didn't seem to study much, his high school buddies say, but his uncanny memory helped him pass tests. And despite Brother Brendan's worries,

Bill's showing his penchant for colorful sweaters.

IN FIRST RACE FOR SCHOOL AND CLUB TODAY

Bill, #10 on the far left, and his brother Pat, #3, third from left, pose in this photo on the eve of the American Schoolboy Rowing Regatta at Ecorse Boat Club, where they would be rowing against schools from across the United States. Be sure to ask Bill who won the race.

Bill graduated in 1950 with a love of mathematics and a high grade-point average – hard to believe for someone who says he never did homework and hated to read because when he read aloud, he'd "mix words backwards and forwards."

"I never read a book until I was 33 years old," Bill says. And that book? "*A Light in the Sink* – it was in the bookcase."

Still, Bill's high school achievements were enough to land him a partial scholarship to the University of Michigan.

Bill never went to college. When he graduated from high school, his parents gave him a power saw. With that, and a cement mixer from Grandpa, he built his first home.

Meanwhile, there was a family to build.

Bill (crouching on far left) with some of his De La Salle classmates prior to graduation.

Bill and Nancy in high school.

Bill – the young father.

Married With 9 Children

The U.S Army drafted Bill during the Korean War, but discharged him after a 21-month stateside tour of duty. Back home, Bill returned to courting his fiancé, a girl he met when she was in high school, the late Nancy Mitchell. They married in 1954. He was 22; she, just months younger.

One of Bill's well-known pranks was "kidnapping" his buddy's wives after they took their vows and returning them after a brief joy ride. When Bill got married, "he knew paybacks were coming," says Dave Kellett. "He had the wedding reception … on Belle Isle. There was one bridge going over, so he was pretty susceptible. But Bill pulled the wool over everybody's eyes. We made the toast and everybody danced. We said, 'Where's Bill and Nancy?' Someone said, 'Come out the back and see.' And he had a boat waiting! … so nobody could get Nancy and steal her.

"He had planned ahead."

Bill always planned ahead, but the children came fast: Four boys and five girls. Nancy gave birth to their first child in 1955, and the last in 1965 – nine over 10 years. There are two sets of "Irish twins," two children born within the same 12-month span.

Like his own father, Bill helped his children make sense of the circumstances of their lives, guiding them to see what was inside each of them and others. He would teach them that sacrifice was a love of a deeper, truer way. Like his father before him, Bill wanted thoughtful, respectful, responsible kids. He wanted them to become independent, know what things cost, and to give freely. And, most importantly, to know that anything – *anything* – was possible.

Bill, influenced by Detroit's automotive culture, thoughtfully explained to one son that, if a person really, really wanted to, he or she could eat a car. It would take time, and one would need to be very aware of how to safely and carefully make it edible, but it was possible, if you set your mind to it.

And, planned for it.

An Atomic Cannon in action in the Nevada desert.

Atomic Bill:
Exploded ... And Demoted

When Bill Pulte makes, or intersects with history — and that happens over and over in his lifetime — the results are often explosive. Never was this more true than after he was drafted at 18 into the U.S. Army and was stationed stateside during the Korean War.

The Atomic Cannon, at 280mm, was the largest U.S. made nuclear-capable mobile artillery. On May 25, 1953, at Frenchman Flat in Nevada, the cannon fired an atomic projectile ... seven miles.

"The 280mm gun is almost the size of a battleship," Bill says. "I was there when we shot off an atomic round."

None of the atomic cannons were ever used in battle since troops couldn't transport the big gun over the Korean mountains. "Eventually they went to Europe and were on the Russian line for 20 years," Bill says.

But for Bill, that wasn't the most eventful happening in his 21-month stint in the service. As a single-stripe Private First-Class, his battery commander demoted him. Bill viewed the dressing-down as one of his best compliments ever.

"You're the only guy in this outfit who can figure out that I'm going to give an order and be five miles away and not have to do it!" barked the commander. "I'm going to bust you down to private. You haven't sewn your stripe on in 45 days!"

"I always enjoyed my life, except for those few months," says Bill. While he loves simplification and systemization, he has always disliked regimentation and rules that don't contribute to the big picture.

Bill (on the right) with two army buddies.

Joanie and Bill.

13 Bedrooms, 10 Baths

When Bill's marriage ended in 1972 and he took on the sole responsibility (with the help of a nanny) for his children, he faced a dilemma: He was raising nine kids ranging in age from 7 to 17 years. He needed a partner.

Next door lived the late Joan McDonald, with her three boys and two girls almost the same ages as the Pultes. Joanie and Bill were struggling with similar child-rearing problems. "So I would go next door," he said. "And ask her what to do in this situation. She was coming over and asking me the same things. All of a sudden we realized: Wait a minute. We're in love."

Bill married "the girl next door." Joan was 41; Bill was 40.

Now the need for simplification, systemization, discipline, and organization increased exponentially as did the need to love 14 kids individually. Kids who had been through considerable early-life changes, and would experience even more in the combined family.

The new home Bill built in Bloomfield Hills, Michigan, had 13 bedrooms and 10 bathrooms. Twelve of the bedrooms were for family, while one was for the nanny. The two youngest boys and two youngest girls each bunked together in separate bedrooms. Everyone else had their own room. Brothers shared bathrooms but each one had his own sink; sisters did the same.

"Joan was a very organized woman," Bill says. "We had two washers and two dryers … 14 compartments in the wall. All clean clothes went in there and had to be emptied by each child every night." If they weren't, there was a penalty.

Bins about a foot square lined a hallway, 10 foot long, between the dining room and kitchen. "Anybody who found anything from any of the kids lying around, they always knew to put it in those bins," Bill says.

Systems like these organized the household. Joan focused on the kids, and Bill was always home for dinner, and the weekend, unless he was out of town on business.

The table was set for 16. "It was buffet style," says Bill. "If you wanted more, you got up and got it. You didn't pass stuff around."

"Joanie ran a tight ship," says a Pulte son. "Dinner was every night at 6:30. If you weren't going to be there for any reason – you had to let her know."

The kids would be fined $2 if they didn't sign out for dinner, a way for their mother to know how much dinner to prepare.

Chores were assigned weekly, on a buddy system. Two kids set the table, two cleaned up and washed dishes. Duty tour rotated every seven weeks. "We always had two kids who worked well together," says Bill. "There were rules any good business would have."

A Birthday A Month

One son remembers his father boosting their confidence by encouraging them to take risks and plan adventures. Like his father before him, Bill taught his children not only to plan, but also to recognize the value of a dollar. This in turn, furthered their confidence.

Every month, a child would plan a Sunday outing: Bowling, a trip to the tourist town of Frankenmuth, a Bob-Lo Excursion Line cruise on the Detroit River, or a Detroit Tigers game. "But you had to plan the entire day," says one Pulte daughter. "You would have to bring him a spreadsheet: How many people were going? How much was it going to cost per person?"

The child in charge of planning the day had to confirm every detail: The event's time, if parking was included in the price, how to get there, whether you needed a reservation, how late the place was open. Farrell's, the ice cream parlor and restaurant, was one frequent destination. "We celebrated many birthdays in there," says a Pulte son. "My dad was always a huge ice cream eater." The kids remember well one of his favorite lines: "I'll have a cheeseburger and strawberry milkshake."

If they spent their allowances and needed something to tide them over, Bill loaned them money at about 5% interest, following Michigan's usury guidelines. An older son undercut his father, however, making loans to the younger kids – at a 4% rate. They made contracts for raking leaves and weeding, specifying hours worked, wages paid, and scheduled completion dates, signed by both parties.

And, yes, there were late fees.

Bill with his favorite dessert.

Because of the demands of 14 kids, Joanie and Bill didn't have as much time as they would have liked with each one. "We weren't at every baseball game," Bill says. "In some ways, I think that gave them more self esteem because they didn't have mom and dad there all the time. They knew it was their job to get there, whether to ask us, or find some other way."

Bill always found ways to make the time he did have with each child memorable and important.

"One of my favorite memories of my dad is when he'd come home after dinner," says one of Bill's sons. "We'd grab my bat and ball and glove and we'd go out in the street, and he'd hit these pop ups and grounders … I just remember and cherish that."

The kids say Bill rarely got angry. He'd emphasize points. And repeat when necessary. *"Do you follow me?"* he'd ask. Or, *"Do you know your costs?"*

"I remember so many times saying, 'I can't do that,'" says one son. "He'd say, 'What the heck do you mean, You can't? There's no such thing as can't.'

"I'd say, 'Dad, I don't know. I'm afraid I might not make it.' He'd say, 'Come on, what are you? Crazy? You're playing as well as anybody out there on the team. You just have to keep plugging. Never give up.'"

While fairness and equality ruled, Bill adjusted what he provided to each individual personality. "He was good at assessing people, what each child needed at different ages," says one of Bill's sons. "He might have said, 'Well, this child needs some discipline or really needs some work on self confidence or something like that.' And he would be able to – without you even realizing it – help in those areas."

Bill wasn't a stickler for examining every report card. He trusted that Joanie, if she was concerned, would bring him problems. He didn't criticize or gossip. He was a firm believer in "freedom with responsibility."

Like his father before him, Bill established traditions. There were funny ones and ones that went straight to the heart.

Joanie made him a jumpsuit, reminiscent of something from Elvis Presley's wardrobe, and he wore it nearly every weekend, judging from the sheer mortification recalled by one child. "He's never been into clothes," she once said – a classic Pulte understatement. Bill's colored or crazily striped or patterned shirts and sweaters light up every Pulte photo album, along with the jumbo ties and the bow ties he wore only at weddings and formal functions.

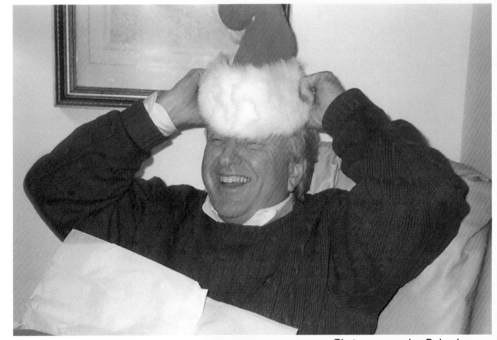

Christmas at the Pulte home.

A son remembers how his Dad carried on the German tradition (still followed in many Pulte families) of wrapping Easter candy in "nests" made of bunched shredded cellophane. Bill, always patient, would hide 10 nests for each child. The nests would then be put in baskets the children also discovered throughout the house.

One Christmas, Bill explained that because they had more than enough of everything, he wanted them to learn about sharing. Everyone groaned when they each received only one present that year. But they used the money that would have been spent on gifts to help out needy families. "We learned the concept of giving our Christmases away," says one Pulte. "Maybe we didn't realize at the time," says another, "but we really had Christmas every day of our lives." It was Bill's plan to share man's sole purpose: To love and be loved.

"He helped shape all our lives for the better," says one of his children. "One of the unique things about dad is many of us feel we were his favorite."

Déjà Vu

When his youngest son, in ninth grade, appealed to him, saying, "Dad, I want to make money," Bill Pulte's thoughts must have flashed back to the time when he sought out his own father for an allowance to gas up his 1939 Plymouth. The search for gas money helped launch his home-building legacy.

But Bill's youngest boy had other things in mind: "I want to shovel snow," he told him.

"Great idea," Bill told his 15-year-old son. "How 'bout if you buy a snow blower? Because if you hand shovel, it will take you two or three days to shovel driveways. I'll lend you $800."

"This was 1977," says his son. At a store on Woodward Avenue, he picked out an inexpensive model, for about $150.

"Your time is worth more," Bill told his son. "Spend the money now. If you buy the right tools and spend the time, you'll be able to get the money back."

Later that week, about $800 in hock, the teenage boy rolled "a huge snow blower" out the door.

"Now, you need a contract," Bill said. So adapting the Pulte Master Builders logo and contracts, his son made agreements headed: Pulte Master Plowers. That deal cost first customer, William J. Pulte, $25 each time it snowed more than three inches.

Bill's son, now a high-end custom builder, learned to buy the right equipment, not to fear investing for a proper return, and that time is worth more than you think. In journals, he logged his oil and gas expenses and the hours it took to blow the snow from each driveway. Bill helped him analyze whether he was charging enough to cover his costs.

After that first year, Bill's son paid back the $800. By the second year, he had enough cash to buy his first used car – a Ford Mustang, the same model Bill drove at the time, though a bit older. From his father he had learned the best way to success: Investing in the product and watching costs for the best chance of a positive outcome …the Pulte Way.

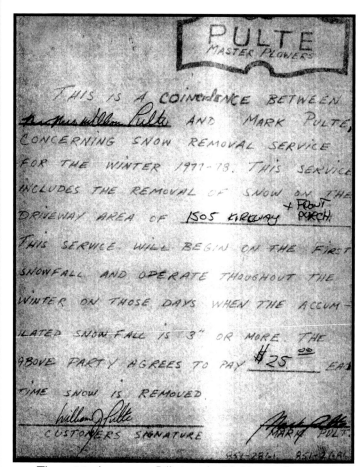

The original contract Bill signed with his son for snow removal.

Welcome Home

Just as when he was a child, Bill begins each day with a morning devotion, attending 8 a.m. mass at Holy Name parish in Birmingham.

Every night he returns home, a quieter home than years ago, for dinner. The front of his house features thick, refurbished doors from a nearly 300 year-old Scottish convent, which he discovered at an antique flea market. Yet, his home is contemporary, beginning with a "floating" foyer bordered by gurgling water. It is a welcome retreat in which to relax his vibrant and open mind. It appeals to his love of layered dimensions.

He kisses his wife, Karen, whom he wed Oct. 2, 1993, and who graciously took on the role of "step-grandmother" to 25 grandchildren. As Karen Koppal, she worked at Pulte Homes for 12 years prior to marrying Bill, so she knew, and loved, his family well.

"Bill enjoys a quiet evening," Karen says, "but he'll be the first to jump up and accept a spontaneous dinner invitation. I am amazed at his energy. There have been times in recent summers while we've been on vacation with family or friends that he's even gone tubing or jet skiing. Would you believe, however, that he still wears his khaki pants and golf shirt!"

And as with his kids, the grandkids keep coming. Each child, as they grow, gets schooled in Pulte wisdom. Bill has been known to ask the next generation, when they start their home-grown businesses: "Ah, hmmm, did you figure out how much this lemonade stand cost?"

Holidays are a challenge to organize these days, since they involve trying to coordinate almost 50 people from around the country. Karen says she plans the Christmas list nearly a year in advance. The table saw, lathe, band saw and drill press in the basement, where Bill once made go-karts and Christmas presents for the kids, are quieter these days, and every now and then, Karen teases Bill about moving them, along with a collection of wire wheels from his old cars.

Karen says Bill has grown more reflective over the past several years, attending both high school and Army reunions. Bill recently was also moved to visit the houses in Ann Arbor where he lived with his parents.

Bill and his son on a jet ski.
Notice the plans in Bill's hands.

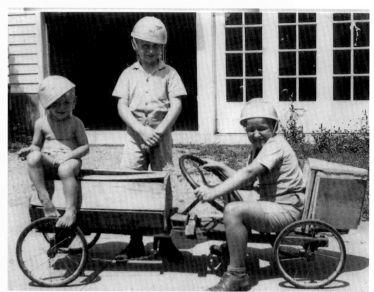

Bill (in the driver's seat) and siblings with an early White Street innovation.

At the house at 1411 White Street, Bill remembered how he, his sister Maureen, and brother Pat, because of either a measles or chicken pox outbreak, were allowed to visit only six houses for Halloween one year. Trick-or-treating quickly finished, they looked at what they had collected on the kitchen table. It was not a good take.

So they traded costumes.

And visited the same houses again.

And again.

The neighbors knew the Pulte kids, but smiled and dropped candy in their sacks anyway, inspired, perhaps, by their ingenuity.

At the next house at 1607 Brooklyn Avenue, Bill recalled the old coal-burning furnace, and how, from the time he was seven years old, it was his job to stoke the "monster," as he and brother Pat, called the thing. It was by the warmth of that furnace that Bill built his first house – a *bird* house. It was for a contest his Grandma Lynch urged him to enter. He remembers sitting in the basement, soldering tiny gutters onto his craft project.

A few years later, Bill would build the real thing, first a cottage in Algonac, Michigan, then a week after graduating high school, the *Detroit Times'* Home No. 103 stock plan, designed by William A. Griffiths, and selected by his mother, from the newspaper.

Even the *Detroit Times'* headline seemed incredulous: "Boy Builds $10,000 House."

The entrepreneurship that flowed from that house, and from the boy who built it, would always, evermore, dwell in family.

Standing in front of 1607 Brooklyn Avenue – Bill remembers tending the "monster" in the basement.

The Kitchen: Losing Your Cookies

Bill's family life, and his experiences with tradesmen who lost time when they had to run off-site to grab a sandwich, gave rise to the "Kitchen" at Pulte headquarters. A place where every home office employee can enjoy lunch every day.

Since the Pulte family mealtime chatter worked to build camaraderie at home, why not borrow that idea to create a home-like, cozy place at work? A place where people could get together?

A snack in the company Kitchen, or in any of the over 50 division offices' break rooms, is somewhat akin to being at home, and that feeling begins with Bill. He wants people to enjoy each other's company and talk – not just about business, but about life: Whose kid helped win the game last night? Who had a new baby? Who caught the flower bouquet at Jill's wedding this weekend?

And Bill's in the kitchen, making a peanut butter-and-jelly sandwich, or enjoying fried chicken, licking his fingers, asking: "How's it going, Joe?" And maybe Joe says, "Not so good." And Bill asks the person he came into the Kitchen with – "Can you excuse me for a couple of seconds?" – and then he's off with Joe.

"He's always in there," says a Pulte employee. "Asking somebody if he or she wants the cookie on their plate, because the rest of them are gone. Talking to people and making sure they're okay. And he'll talk to everyone … especially if they have an idea about how to make the culture better, how to make the company better: 'What can we do?'"

The Kitchen has proven to be a place for everyone to stand on equal footing. It doesn't matter if you're a vice president or a manager or a secretary. It's one reason why our corporate culture is strong. Sometimes, we really do feel like we're at home.

Karen and Bill.

Karen Pulte helps keep Bill young at heart. Bill, meanwhile, is her rock.

Following a discrete courtship, Karen Koppal married William J. Pulte the 3rd on Oct. 2, 1993. They took a three-week European honeymoon that Bill personally planned down to the finest detail. Having never traveled outside of the United States, Karen packed in preparation for any eventuality.

After lugging three large suitcases in and out of some of Europe's most famous cities, Karen says, "That first experience quickly taught me how to pack and how not to pack." In contrast, Bill is monastic in his packing methods, surviving most business trips with socks and essentials.

Since then, however, travel has become an important part of Bill and Karen's life together. They've even been to Egypt, where Bill, never one to shirk a new experience, wasted no time in climbing atop a camel.

Karen says she is amazed at Bill's resiliency and outlook. "He laughs at things I get frustrated with, and I am amazed at the willingness with which he takes them on," she says. "He has been a pillar in my life."

Karen, too, has had an influence on Bill. Several years his junior, she has made him more aware of life beyond work as evidenced by the increasing time they spend with family and friends. They even go to rock concerts together – evidence of Bill's openness to new experiences.

Another significant influence Karen has had on Bill concerns his wardrobe. "I'm always a little concerned when I'm not around to consult on what he's wearing. He'll go to the office, and employees will say, 'Uh-oh, Karen's out of town,'" she says.

Karen doesn't worry about cooking for Bill. "I'm a consumer, not a connoisseur," he tells her. Playing golf with him, she's learned his love of the lost golf ball. "He never really challenged the alligators, but I think he did snakes," she says. "He's a golfer and fisherman. That's what people say about him on the course."

In 1998, with Bill's kids, Karen sponsored her husband in the Phoenix Pro-Am, and he won 3rd place, with a handicap of 15. Bill hit a ball into the rough, and eager to retrieve it (as always), quickly learned about jumping cactus. Brushing against a Chainfruit Cholla, a barbed spine stuck in his hand. "That taught him a lesson," Karen says. Over the years, Bill has played golf with Fred Funk, David Duval, and Steve Jones.

While he says he learns a great deal from her, Karen responds by saying how her spiritual life has deepened significantly since her marriage to Bill.

"I am nowhere near where he is," she says. "He has taught me a lot about God, family, faith, love, charity, and forgiveness and fairness ... Because of him I am a better person."

*"Everybody at Pulte
calls me Bill.
There's no Mr. Pulte."*

At the Phoenix Pro-Am Tournement, Bill experiences the Jumping Cholla cactus.

Chapter Two
The Entrepreneur

B ill Pulte always had a plan.

Bill the builder — his trusty
Plymouth in the background.

But on one June day in 1950, he didn't have a plumber.

Bill needed the plumber for his first house, the house featured in the *Detroit Times*. The plumber's job was first: Tap the sewer and water lines, and run pipe to the basement. So Bill needed the plumber to pull a permit before he received the authorization to build.

The plumber's office closed at 4:30 p.m. Bill had little time to spare. He tore through the city in his '39 Plymouth.

"On the way from the east side to the west side, I got caught in a funeral line," he recalls.

"I had to get out.

"So I'm over the yellow line, the center line, and traffic is coming at me. I have to duck around. I clip a car. And I realize: *I caused an accident.* Not a big accident, no one was hurt, but I pull over to the curb. And they called the police from a gas station."

The policeman wrote Bill six tickets: Reckless driving, obstructing a funeral line, driving on the wrong side of the street, causing an accident – those are the four that Bill remembers.

He got to the plumber's in time. But imagine how the traffic violations clipped his profits on that first, $10,000 home.

Some might argue Bill's story as an entrepreneur began when he sold his first quart of cherries from his mother's backyard tree. Or, when he went to his dad for gas money, and his father suggested he find a way to earn it. Or, when he was fired from his first lawn-mowing job. While moping around a bit, his Grandma Lynch gently suggested that, at 16, he should become a carpenter's helper.

Was Bill's entrepreneurship formed while he perspired on a hot roof and saw his builder employer drive up in his new Cadillac, a glass of iced tea shimmering on the dashboard?

Perhaps.

But, in that race across the city, Bill *made it happen*. Taking risks – some he'd never take again (no tickets since) – with determined, single-minded purpose, he signed the contract that would launch his first truly entrepreneurial business venture.

Six citations and a funeral later, he left the plumber's office with a $650 deal and the knowledge that his subcontractor would soon get him started. Now, his money – though on loan from the same aunt who owned his building lot – was *in*. "Unless you've got your own money in, you're not an entrepreneur," Bill says today.

Picture the smile on his face in June 1950, even with those tickets stuffed in his pocket.

At 18, *that day*, he became *William J. Pulte, BUILDER.*

"Unless you've got your own money in, you're not an entrepreneur."

> *"I guess I was
> an entrepreneur
> from the time
> I was five."*

Bill's Absolutes

Because of his ingrained modesty, we'll never read about Bill in an Encyclopedia of the American Entrepreneur, or see his wax replica wearing a multi-colored sweater in an Entrepreneurial Museum.

But the genius is real.

The story of the birth of Bill's entrepreneurial instincts is as elaborate as the story of his family life.

Fifty-three years after that harried cross-town ride, on November 10, 2003, *Forbes* magazine wrote: *Pulte's genius has been to decipher the psychology of consumers' home-buying decisions in nearly every market segment.*

Bill admits the fireplace he built in his five-room bungalow back in 1950 was, perhaps, one extra too many for the neighborhood. But the house, still, deciphered the psychology of the market. The fireplace – adjacent to the front door – drew attention. Bill sold the place before the job was complete.

"All the things Bill was good at years ago as an individual are the very same things we are good at now as a company," says a Pulte executive. "He could be, and should be, in an entrepreneurial Hall of Fame. He has the classic traits: He risked it all. He bet big. He won."

And that's only for his contribution to the craft of home building and land development. Bill has contributed much more than that. He's developed many innovative and committed leaders. Leaders who possess diverse talents while sharing Bill's vision and values.

His insights include not merely defining customers, but always seeking ways to provide greater value, reduce costs, and speed production. At the same time, he has developed a company that, through decentralized divisions, continues to foster an entrepreneurial mindset.

Bill unearthed these principles in his early days: Have a plan. Take calculated risks. Diversify, both geographically and in product mix. If it ain't broke, yes, fix it. Surround yourself with smart people who are loaded with common sense.

Bill applied creative solutions to problems and not only embraced change, but also preempted it.

You can't appreciate where Bill Pulte has come from until you hear the stories of his earliest days sandwiched between reminiscences of family, friends, and business partners.

Maureen Sheehan, Bill's only sister, shares some of the most poignant and vivid stories. Maureen recalls a time when she was helping him paint the interior of his second home, built for their parents.

"He had an old truck," she says. "And he and I would go to the house on Buckingham in this old truck. It had a hole in the floor under my feet. It would be raining, and he'd go over puddles. The water would splash up on me and we would be singing."

Picture that: Bill, driving like the dickens, springs of the old truck seat jabbing him, rain pouring down, water splashing through the floor-boards. Despite the rain, despite the rickety truck – with their hope for the future lodged in their hearts – the two of them laughing and singing an old Mario Lanza song.

While Bill would never be known for his singing, he could make a great peanut butter and jelly sandwich. Maureen recalls sitting on the unfinished kitchen floor, surrounded by paint cans, eating peanut butter and jelly for lunch, the two of them, their hands speckled with paint.

Bill's entrepreneurial streak started long before that wet, ear-splitting truck ride. Not because he was overly troubled by the fact that a second-hand bicycle was all his parents could afford at Christmas – "I knew my mother and father tried their best" – but because he "wanted to have a 'new something.'"

"I guess I would say I was an entrepreneur from the time I was 5," Bill says. "I lived about three-quarters of a mile from the Michigan football stadium in Ann Arbor. My father let my brother and I fill up our yard every Saturday. For 25 cents a car … we got 10 to 15 cars in there."

Bill sold the *Saturday Evening Post* door-to-door, Christmas cards, greeting cards, cherries picked from backyard trees. "Every pint of cherries I picked for my mother, I got to pick a quart for myself and sell them door to door," he says. He built, and sold, 15 ping-pong tables, and kayaks from a kit in *Mechanics Illustrated*. To his surprise and dismay, Bill later learned that one kayak was used by a thief, who was arrested by police on the Huron River.

An early Pulte "crew." Bill's father, wearing the hat, is standing alongside the truck with Bill's brother Tim. Another brother, Bob, is in the back of the truck.

Setbacks became comebacks. He learned the value of first-name familiarity, and loyalty. His love of the trades and his requirement that his leaders share that love, would match his passion for clarity. He'd embrace innovation.

Like any entrepreneur, he'd make mistakes – starting with that first home. But unlike many, he'd *embrace* mistakes, with no visible ego. He'd never be afraid to admit the truth.

Humility is an improbable stepping stone to success, yet, at Pulte Homes, it may be the keystone to the company's success. It's one of the philosophies Bill employed as an entrepreneur that could apply to any business, in any industry.

The principles he taught his children would apply, too, in his business: *Always* know your costs. *Never* be afraid to ask dumb questions. Stupid questions and smarter people helped him build his legacy, beginning at 11451 Christy Street in Detroit.

Early Experts: Mom, Dad, Carlo

It was on job sites at age 16 that Bill's ideals took shape. Carlo Bartonio, his boss, was an Italian mason. Over time, Carlo became a home builder, and while he computed measurements in his head faster than anyone, Bill later figured out that the 1947 immigrant to the United States couldn't read or write English. So on visits to the lumberyard, Bill was Carlo's "interpreter."

Bill inundated Carlo with questions, all patiently answered.

"He'd ask the dumbest questions you ever thought about in your life," says Dave Kellett, Pulte's first construction vice president. "I'm sure as he walked away, these old Italians would say, 'Boy there's one dumb kid.' He wasn't afraid of what they thought. He wanted to understand. Once he got the answer in his head, it was imprinted there."

After Carlo drove up to a jobsite in his new Cadillac one day, with a glass of iced tea on the dash, Bill, hot and sweaty on a roof, but enjoying his suntan, wiped his brow and somehow figured he knew enough to become a tradesman builder, too.

Bill secured a 50 x 120-foot lot from his father's sister, Marcella, promising to pay her $2,000 when he sold the house for $10,000. The house plan was one his

"I always had a plan. I didn't know they called it strategy back then, but I always knew where I was going."

mother selected from the *Detroit Times'* House of the Week section. But, he then learned from the Permits Office that he needed to be 21 years old to build a house for sale.

He drove home deep in thought.

Like his Halloween costume switch, back in Ann Arbor when he was a kid, he returned to the Permits Office the next day, undeterred. He told the same permit official he was going to build the house … for himself.

Because of the plumbing requirement, he requested bids from six plumbers. Over 19 days, he received bids ranging from $1,250 to $1,875. Dismayed, as the high bid was nearly the lot's price, he turned to his dad, his second expert (mom being the first), who suggested a third: Carlo.

"He's not very smart," the teenager told his dad. "Why would I go to him?"

"Well if he's not so smart," said Bill's father, "why is he building more houses now than when you worked for him?"

"I swallowed my 18-year-old genius pride and decided to go see Carlo," says Bill.

In 10 seconds flat, the builder flipped through Bill's four-page plan. "Plumbing cost should be $625 for that deal," he told the younger tradesman-builder. Carlo also recommended the right plumber.

After waiting nearly three weeks for bids, and facing the possibility that, with the high number, his plumbing costs could have driven him to bankruptcy, Bill witnessed, in less than 11 seconds, his former employer cut his costs by two-thirds. From that day forward, he checked all his pricing with his Italian-American mentor.

"After that first house, I decided I was going to be thinking and planning and let others do the construction."

Boy Builds $10,000 House

WILLIAM PULTE III, ONLY 18, PAINTING THE HOUSE HE BUILT HIMSELF
... *"building was to be my life work. I was too impatient to go to college"* ...

Gives Up College to Be Contractor

By E. A. BATCHELOR

A four-room bungalow, built with his own hands and already sold for $10,000, stands at 11451 Christy to prove that William Pulte III, 18, already is eminently qualified for the builder's license which he cannot obtain for three years.

Young Pulte started his project back in mid-August.

Work on the house, nearing completion today, was done by young Pulte and two friends except the foundation, the electrical wiring and the plumbing.

He says modestly that he might have been able to do the electricity and plumbing too, but a city ordinance insists that they be done by licensed contractors.

HELPED GRANDFATHER

While the physical work only started in mid-August the idea probably was born 10 years ago when Bill, already fascinated by the building trade, was allowed to help his grandfather, a contractor, with light tasks.

He has worked every summer vacation since, each year rating more skilled assignments.

Last year at the Detroit Builders Show young Pulte bought the plans for The Detroit Times Home No. 103, designed by William A. Griffiths.

CAUGHT MISTAKES

"Fortunately I was able to discover most of my mistakes and correct them before they were too far advanced.

"For example I found my stairway was too narrow and had to rip part of the rough work out and start over."

Bill, who lives at 14302 Rosemary, plans a larger house as his next project. Not having a license he must build the homes for himself and then sell them.

Young Pulte, a husky 160-

2 Young Friends Are His Crew

honor student. Bill had a chance for a college scholarship but turned it down explaining

"I had made up my mind years before that building was going to be my life's work. I was too impatient to get started to go to college."

BUILT COTTAGE

Bill first tried his wings last June when, assisted by two classmates, Dave Kellett and Jim Youngblood, he built a cottage in Algonac.

With this practise venture out of the way he drew out his savings of approximately $2,000 and borrowed some more from his father and began his undertaking.

Bill purchased the lot from a relative. He let out the foundation digging to a sub-contractor. Then, with Kellett and Youngblood supplying the unskilled

Bill's first house – as reported in the *Detroit Times*.

Bill hired an excavator to dig the basement, and both he and a high school buddy helped the mason build the foundation. Three more friends helped him frame the house, and he paid them $1 an hour. "I should have hired framers," Bill says. "My buddies bent so many nails it cost me way more than it should."

By September, his nail-benders were college-bound. Bill roofed and sided the Christy Street bungalow himself. A *Detroit Times* photographer snapped him outside on a ladder. He painted it alone and laid the oak floor. "If you didn't hit your nail right, you hit your fingernails," he says. "I was all black and blue. I was holding the last nails with pliers."

The house fared a little better than his hands. Some would note Bill put the driveway on the wrong side, opposite the side door. William J. Pulte, BUILDER, told the *Detroit Times*: "I was able to discover most of my mistakes and correct them before they were too far advanced."

One house was sufficient, however, for Bill to ditch his plan to be a tradesman builder. "After the first house, I decided I was going to be thinking and planning and let others do the construction," he says.

For his second house, a colonial for his parents, he used a line of credit negotiated from a mason supply house operated by Bill Back. Admiring the young man's guts, he told Bill he'd stand as a reference for anyone calling about the Pulte line of credit. Leveraging Mr. Back's leap of faith, Bill secured credit lines at Damman Hardware, assuring the owners he would reward their trust with loyalty.

Bill hired an architect, the late Bob Wood, who "designed more Pulte homes than anybody in the United States," Bill says. He paid him $25 for his parent's house plans, which he built in Detroit's Grosse Pointe suburb.

This time, carpenters and masons did the heavy work, although Bill still nailed shingles and poured the basement floor. His sister, Maureen, helped paint. "If I made money on the first house, I lost it on this one," he says.

Meanwhile, Bill was watching what other Detroit builders were doing. Soon after World War II had ended, Miller Homes and Edward Rose & Sons were building 500 houses a year. They were becoming, as he saw them, the first entrepreneurial builders – businessmen who ran a company and directed the trades.

There was high demand for housing after the war and banks were interested in making the earliest GI bill loans to home buyers, funneling business to entrepreneurs like Rose.

"Bill Levitt out on the East Coast was probably the first production builder," Bill says. "He was building, during the war, barracks in mass production. He'd put barracks up almost overnight." Now, Levitt was adopting the same methods to bring houses to post-war Baby Boomers.

About the same time William J. Levitt was making a name for himself in New York and Pennsylvania with his modular, ranch-style houses, William J. Pulte decided he wanted to be Detroit's best custom builder, working from architect-specified plans. He did well, and built a home for a top Ford executive. Then, he learned he was low bidder on a house planned for Benson Ford, grandson of Ford founder Henry Ford.

The architect told him he did marvelous work: "Any other family but the Ford family, I'd give you this job. But I can't afford to risk my reputation on a 24-year-old kid."

"At 24, I was even more of a genius than I was at 18," Bill says. "It took me until I was 30 to realize how dumb I was. The architect was probably right. I would have had to import that marble from Italy and get the faucets from Spain. And I had a hard enough time getting stuff from the local hardware store."

He didn't get any tickets on the drive home that day, but decided architects were not going to run his business. Commercial contracting was where he was heading. He changed his plan.

"The architect said, 'Bill, there's no question. If it was any other family but the Ford family, I'd give you this job. I can't afford to risk my reputation on a 24-year-old kid.'"

> *"As soon as you know you can't do something you've agreed to, you need to tell the party and work it out now, not when it's past. This is being true to your word."*

Early on, two real estate developers adopted Bill as a "pseudo son." "One lent me money when I periodically needed it," Bill says.

"In the 1950s, $10,000 was the same as $100,000 today," Bill says. "Getting money in the early days was one of my toughest problems. But he would lend me money and I always told him when I could pay it back, which was the day after I was going to close."

On one particular house, Bill learned the closing was going to be postponed for three weeks. Bill said OK, and didn't do anything. He paid the money he owed the day after the closing.

But when he asked to borrow another $10,000, his financier said no.

"You paid it three weeks late," he told Bill. "The customer is not between you and me. You could have come to me and said, 'I'm going to be three weeks late.' I'm telling you, as soon as you know that you can't make a given date, you better tell your lender you can't make it."

Says Bill: "He taught me a lesson worth millions of dollars because I went back early enough to people, so they said: 'Don't worry. Bill Pulte is ahead of the game in telling us he can't do it. But we'll work it out.'

"It was a great lesson, but it was a real setback at the time."

Bill learned to be true to his word. He learned to tell people when something wouldn't work and when he'd make it work.

The GM of Home Builders

By 1957, Bill had hired his high school buddy Dave Kellett as his first full-time employee, a superintendent. Earlier, he had hired a part-time secretary.

He thought building factories, churches, schools, and shopping centers promised better margins. He learned the truth. "Even today, general contractors work on half the margin that a small builder does to build a house," Bill says.

He also noticed tradesmen on commercial jobs shared no "family feeling." Building houses, workmen were proud of their craft. If they nicked a wall or edge, they'd say something to the other guy and trade repairs. With commercial work, tradesmen came and went. Camaraderie didn't exist. "That's when I realized maybe I ought to be developing my own lots and building my houses," Bill says.

Dave Kellett remembers Bill telling him he wanted to create a company recognized as the "General Motors of Home Builders." GM built automobiles for a variety of market segments and advertised superb engineering, solid construction, and comfortable rides. Bill, likewise, put thought and research into making sure homes were well crafted and designed. (By then, he had figured out that side doors work best when they are adjacent to driveways.) He had mentors in real estate who shared rules for interior and architectural design.

In 1959, he bought the land for his first subdivision, 50 lots, thinking he would target the earliest move-up buyers. He became his own land developer.

"I decided I would go directly to the farmer myself, buy the land, develop it, and then sell it," Bill says. "This made it more profitable."

While he had great rapport with subcontractors, he didn't have money to pay them. He told his trades he'd pay as he sold homes. He was going to sell 10 to 12 a month, or so he pledged.

He didn't know it then, but under his new plan, Bill was about to embark on the ride of his life.

Bill Pulte and Joe Baranska examining a model of a 320-acre diversified community for Farmington Township, Michigan. Their new concept upset community officials and planning commissions. Bill convinced the officials that his plan would work . . . and it did.

120 Days: 2 Homes Sold

When 120 days passed and he had sold only two homes in Concord Green, his first subdivision, Bill wondered: "What's wrong?"

The tract was at the end of an isolated dirt road in West Bloomfield Township, just miles from Pulte Homes' headquarters today. Bill hired his old high school buddy Joe Baranska, a real estate broker, to help him figure out a marketing solution while Bill determined what was wrong with the houses themselves.

Bill, Joe, and Dave Kellett took a trip East, staying in one hotel room, flipping a coin for who got the cot, and learning a few things about production housing. North of Philadelphia, they waited in line for two hours to tour a William J. Levitt house. Levittown, Pennsylvania opened Bill's eyes.

"Levittown was a miracle," Bill says. "He did so many things speedy-fast, production-wise. After I saw this, I knew mass production could be done, easily."

It was all based on scheduling, he observed. Levitt had a schedule, and stuck to it. "And he had a volume of buyers so when they came off the assembly line, he had somebody to take them," Bill says.

Levitt's modular housing utilized preassembled factory framing, erected on site and finished with drywall, wiring and plumbing. Foundations were site-built. In the 1980s, Bill Pulte would advance Levitt's concept, with panelization, to save time and money and maintain precision quality. Bill experimented with framed, pre-wired walls, with drywall – assembled in factories, concrete basement walls, and staircases. Even later, some of Pulte's million-dollar homes would use factory components.

But again, we're getting ahead of our story.

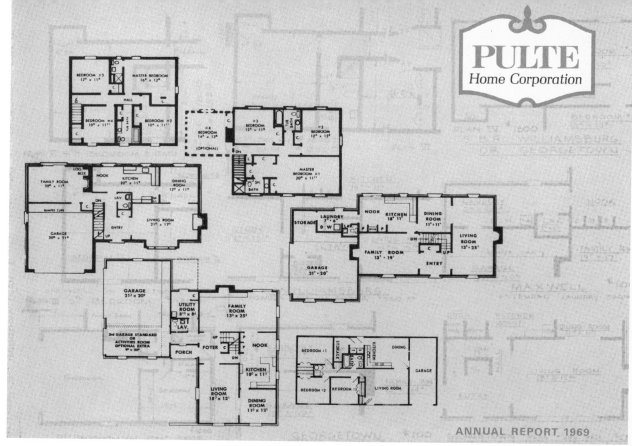

A Pulte home plan featured in the company's 1969 Annual Report.

"Building was to be my life's work. I was too impatient to go to college."

Bill visited other builders around the country who were targeting move-up buyers. Used to building custom homes, he realized too much customization was going into his product; once more, as with his first home, the two models for the neighborhood were overbuilt.

Bill had brought back with him several of Levitt's slick marketing brochures but decided that wasn't the way he wanted to go. Always thinking a step ahead, he decided to take a leap forward and build models buyers could see and feel. While he was among the first, if not *the* first production builder to show model homes, the first two models he built didn't sell, he says. "I had to chuck them and build two more," he recalls.

The lessons learned, however, allowed him to reduce each home's cost while, at the same time, increasing the size of the home by 100 square feet. This change prompted the motto: *"Pulte offers the most square footage for the money."*

Joe Baranska remembers the tough, early days. He went his first week without a paycheck. Dave Kellett tells another story, about Bill's bookkeeper, named Jeanette. "We were in the basement of one of the model homes," he says. "Joe turned to Jeanette and asks: 'Do you have a paper clip?' Jeanette snapped back: 'What happened to the two I gave you yesterday?'"

In Six Months: 45 Homes Sold

On "the sale that was going to save us" Joe Baranska remembers one home buyer saying: "I noticed you have only one outlet on the side of the door. I'd like to have two, so they're balanced."

Bill insisted: "That's $10."

"No, you don't understand," the home buyer said. "I'm buying this expensive house. Throw it in."

"If you want it, it's $10," Bill said, firmly.

("I would have given that guy $100!" Joe Baranska says today.)

"I'm not going to buy the house," the home buyer said, stomping out the door.

"My God!" Joe said to Bill. "We needed that sale desperately."

"Don't worry," Bill said. "He'll be back."

And he was.

He bought the home the next day.

But the principle was established: Bill knew they were building a quality product that provided great value and so he wasn't afraid to take a calculated risk. It was a pattern he would repeat again and again.

Bill took risks with marketing as well. He had to, because he had bare-bones budgets, and in the case of Concord Green, he was working in a town that prohibited fixed signage.

*"Don't worry.
He'll be back."*

Joe Baranska suggested taking a car and parking it on the corner with a sign. "That's a great idea," Bill told him. "Why don't we get a bunch of cars?"

They bought 12 junkers for $50 each and painted them green, along with Joe's and Bill's cars. Atop the cars, triangular signs read "Concord Green." Each car's bumper held an enlarged photo of the model. They parked the cars all over the city, in gas stations, and in front of competitors' new houses.

In six months, they sold 45 homes. "That is when Pulte really started to be the company it is today," Bill says.

The two new models won *McCall's* magazine's House of the Year awards. For months afterward, the company received home plan requests, and sold them for $50 – paper clips included.

It was the result of re-worked plans and creative marketing – a combination that produced a solution that would become an essential ingredient of Pulte success.

It was 1960. Bill Pulte had become a production builder.

PHOTOGRAPH BY HEDRICH-BLESSING. DRAW

$21,950 in Michigan*

"It looks the way a house should look!" "Now, there is a house with real elegance!" "But it's truly charming!" So go the comments about this delightful, well-planned Southern Colonial house. It has old-time charm coupled with such modern conveniences as a family room, sliding glass doors, built-in oven, a full dining room, large closets, and master-bedroom suite; a fourth bedroom, over the garage, is optional. The house has a full basement, wood paneling in the family room, wardrobe-type closets, and underground utilities eliminating telephone and electricity poles. And, of course, it is a Certified House.

When a house is Certified by McCALL's, the plans and specifications have been approved by a jury of editors, architects, building experts, and women delegates to McCall's Congress on Better Living. *Cost of the house, without land, in Bloomfield, Michigan. Cost to duplicate it may be somewhat higher or lower in your community, depending on local conditions.

For a complete list of builders of homes that have been certified by McCALL's, write: Director, Home Certification Program, McCall's, 230 Park Avenue, New York 17, New York.

Builder: William J. Pulte, Inc., Bloomfield, Michigan
Area: 2,350 square feet, plus garage

68

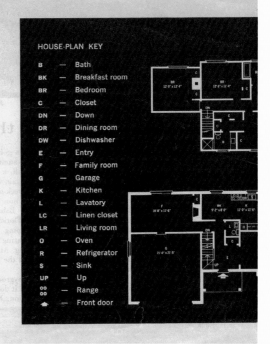

HOUSE-PLAN KEY

B	—	Bath
BK	—	Breakfast room
BR	—	Bedroom
C	—	Closet
DN	—	Down
DR	—	Dining room
DW	—	Dishwasher
E	—	Entry
F	—	Family room
G	—	Garage
K	—	Kitchen
L	—	Lavatory
LC	—	Linen closet
LR	—	Living room
O	—	Oven
R	—	Refrigerator
S	—	Sink
UP	—	Up
OO OO	—	Range
◆	—	Front door

Pulte Homes wins *McCall's* House of the Year award.

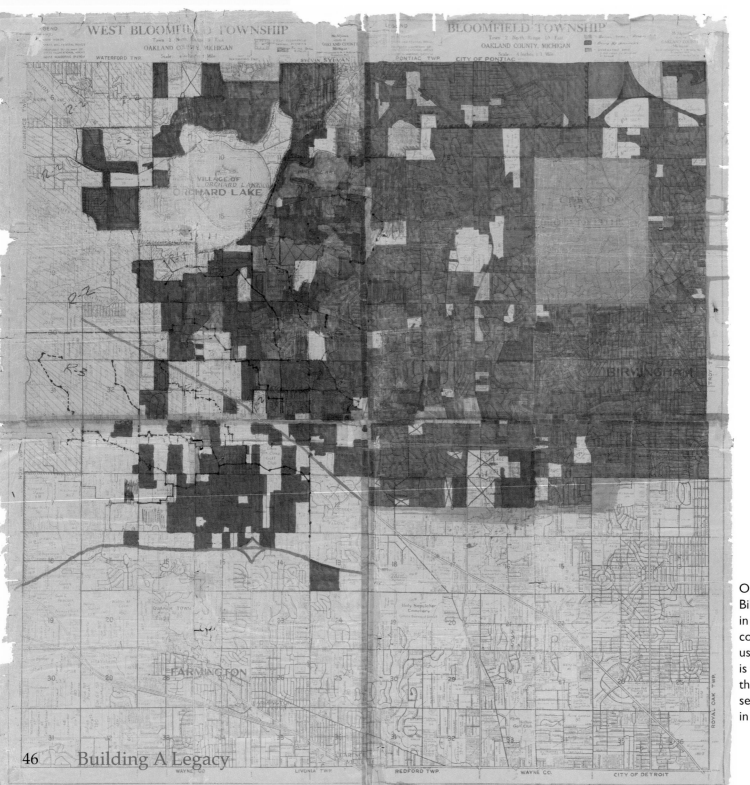

On this 1958 map, we can see Bill's plans for land acquisition in a Michigan community. Each color represents a different land use (as defined by Bill). The map is fondly remembered as marking the beginning of Pulte's "market segmentation" work that is used in every Pulte division today.

Building A Legacy

A Green, Orange And White Future

Pulte Homes maintains a famous artifact: A tattered, old map of West Bloomfield and Bloomfield Townships. Now somewhat faded, it was colored in green, orange, and white to designate different land uses. Bill used this map to target various land parcels for potential purchase.

"We'd take and divide every metropolitan area into submarkets," says Bill. To be successful in production home building, Bill knew he had to excel at determining: Who? From Where? Would Pay How Much? And, For What?

"Bill had an inexplicable ability to pick the right land," says Joe Baranska. "He would draw a circle around the best location, the best school district, and then go out and look for land in a specific location."

Joe says Bill's methods magnified his uncanny knack for buying prime development sites. In one case, in a move that others thought was ill-advised, he bought property across the street from a sewage plant. Then the plant shut down. "They made an art museum out of it, and we sold houses like they were going out of style," says Joe.

The Pulte saying, "Our Product: A House on a Lot in a Community," evolved from Bill's understanding that homebuyers didn't just want a roof over their heads, they wanted a safe, convenient, attractive neighborhood. They wanted the same sense of belonging Bill craved when he was growing up on Brooklyn Avenue.

Families wanted space, too. Pulte's floor plans increased living space, typically adding family rooms, a feature many builders didn't offer at the time. Instead of the usual 10x10-foot den and standard bath, Pulte built 15x14-foot libraries, and deluxe bathrooms. Dave Kellett recalls other trips he and Joe and Bill made to California, where design trends seemed to germinate, to look at new homes, "so we'd be a step ahead of everybody."

The company built its second and third subdivisions.

On another trip, the three men saw the remarkable job Kettler Brothers did in Washington, D.C., particularly when it came to merchandising and decorating homes. But, of more interest to Bill than seeing how homes were being marketed, was learning how in other regions of the country the economy could be different.

Right People: Taking The Walk With Bill

From the beginning, everyone shared in Bill Pulte's success.

That's due to Bill's ability to partner with the right people, particularly trade contractors and suppliers.

"Bill was able to convince people who were good and shared his vision, that under the high production model, with less frills, they would make less per house, but the volume they'd generate would more than make up for any lost margin," says a Pulte executive.

Those who jumped on board with Bill, in five to 10 years, had businesses that were phenomenally successful. Bill developed these relationships in Colorado, Detroit, Atlanta, Chicago, and Washington, D.C. Many still stand today.

"And I'm talking about everyone from small tradesmen up to some of the largest plumbing contractors in Chicago or Detroit," the executive says. "All because they took that walk with Bill, and understood what it was like to be a production subcontractor."

Detroit's economy was sagging. "It was a one-horse market," Bill says. "The automobile was king. When the automobile wasn't selling, we weren't selling homes. Washington, D.C. had never heard the word recession."

In late 1963, Bill began his geographic diversification when he bought a subdivision for 500 houses, called Fox Hills, in Potomac, Maryland, outside Washington, D.C., now one of the most established, exclusive suburbs of the city. A Pulte home in Fox Hills bought for $35,000 now can sell for more than $1 million.

This sort of diversification saved Pulte many times. "I didn't lose a beat in most of the recessions because they weren't nationwide," Bill says.

Change *Before* It's Broken

"Never be afraid to make changes," the Pulte founder says. The tradesman-builder turned custom-builder turned commercial-contractor turned entrepreneurial-production-builder should know. "The worst advice I ever got was, 'If it ain't broke, don't fix it.' *Everything* is changing. *All the time.* If you're in the computer business and took that attitude, you'd have been bankrupt years ago."

Never was this truer than when Bill began building outside Washington – his new sandbox.

The day before he opened his Fox Hills models, he was helping his interior decorator hang pictures and drapery, because he couldn't afford to hire anyone to help. He'd invested everything he owned in the community, even mortgaged his own home.

"We were all exhausted," Bill says. "We forgot lunch, we were so excited to get these three models done. It was Friday night and we're going out the front door. Who should come in but my banker, actually a mortgage guy. The big lenders back in those days were the life insurance companies.

"'Bill!' the man said. 'Would you mind taking me through?'

"What am I gonna tell him?" says Bill. "No? I owed him something like 50 million bucks at that point. So I take him through. I'm excited. I'm showing him this and that.

'Well, they look nice,' the financier says. 'But they won't sell.'

"Everything is changing. All the time. Look how many people have changed history because it wasn't broke but they did fix it."

The Pulte Homes Fox Hills development
in suburban Washington, D.C.

"I mean, I've got every *dime* I could borrow in this community, and he's telling me *it's nice but it won't sell?*"

The banker ticks off 10 reasons, among them: Windows are too big. There's too many. The poured basement walls weren't cement block, which home buyers liked. Instead of the block local builders used for exterior walls, Bill had used framing lumber and insulation, and, instead of running ceramic bath tile up the wall four feet, Bill had tiled the floor and a low base. In some homes, he built half basements.

"I'm selling 300 or 400 houses a year in Detroit all with poured basements," Bill tells the banker. "I can insulate framed walls a lot better than block, and I can build my houses cheaper. And, faster."

"Won't sell," the man says.

"I listened for a minute," Bill says. "But I was really kind of depressed."

Turned out, the banker was dead wrong.

Four years later, every builder in Washington, D.C., was building the Pulte Way. The 10 reasons for impending failure, as the banker saw it, practically became construction standards. Bill's methods cut cost, improved quality, increased perceived value, and sped production.

"That was a risk," says Bill. "It was a very serious risk. But I figured it's got to be common-sense."

Now he had a new slogan: *Pulte Built is Better Built.*

Going Public: A People Strategy

By 1964, expansion to D.C. drove sales to $9 million. In 1966, Pulte moved into Chicago, and in 1968, into Atlanta.

By 1969, sales nudged $24 million. Now, not only were Pulte homes in demand, but Bill discovered that his people and their expertise were, too.

"I had this team of people in four cities," says Bill. "And these guys were being offered twice the money I was giving them. So I went to my attorney and said, 'Is there some way we could design a profit-sharing program for these guys so I can keep them?'"

After serious consideration, he decided the only way to do that was to take the company public, offering Pulte stock on Wall Street. The move would allow employees to buy stock, originally Bill's stock, at a discount, making it a profit-sharing plan.

About seven builders had preceded Bill into the stock market, including Bill Levitt and U.S. Home. "Home builders back then were little bitty companies," Bill says. Some went public to eliminate having to obtain interim construction financing. Others, to raise capital for expansion.

Bill had his own reason: *To keep people*.

Bill (second from right) and his team on the floor of the New York Stock Exchange.

Never Too Late To *Reverse*

Bill Pulte's entrepreneurial mindset means he never perceives an unforeseen circumstance, or a calculated risk that didn't pan out, as a failure.

In the early 1980s, when the United States government bailed out Chrysler, there was little job growth and Detroit was hurting, along with its housing market. Bill Pulte decided as chairman of the board to do the unthinkable: Shut down the Michigan division, and sell the land it controlled. It was a decision he never truly embraced.

He knew his land positions were good positions, and that the economy would revive.

"The key to home building is to control the right land," Bill says. "That's the only product I can't buy off the shelf. It's the only product that takes a lot of time to process, a lot of time to go from the farmer's field to a subdivision."

Two years later, he bought the same Detroit land back, at higher prices, and restarted the division.

The moral of the story: Great land is great land – even if the economy fluctuates, the value of land always increases. Today a key component of the company's business strategy is to maintain control of hundreds of thousands of lots.

After Pulte Homes went public, it continued its expansion into other markets. Product diversification, with first-time buyer housing funded through Federal Housing Authority and Veteran Affairs loans, lay ahead, as would the creation of a mortgage subsidiary to better serve buyers.

Leadership decisions became critical as Bill grew his company, made acquisitions, and became, through education and training, an employer and company no competitor could beat in either corporate culture or product.

Pulte's quick reaction to consumer preferences, economic cycles, and geographic housing demands made it possible to continue years of profitability – again, due to its people.

And Bill would rely on these people more and more as Pulte became a formidable competitor like no other.

A competitor, whose founder, as a boy out of high school, tore across town in an old car, with a fresh plan, and no plumber.

"I didn't have any money. My parents couldn't give me any, so I had to figure out how to earn it."

Chapter Three
The Competitor

"The most easily copied thing in our business is our houses," says Bill Pulte. "What the competition *can't* copy is our people."

When Bill took the company public in 1969, the same summer Neil Armstrong walked on the moon, his aspiration was to accomplish something more down to earth yet just as visionary. His competitive drive was as strong as President John F. Kennedy's vision of beating the Soviets to that lofty real estate.

"This is, whether we like it or not … a race," Kennedy said. "Being second to the moon is nice, but it's … like being second anytime."

Bill wasn't taking on Russian cosmonauts, he was competing against other builders, who had taken their companies public to fund geographic and product expansion.

And like President Kennedy, he had no intention of giving way.

His step onto new ground, however, was to become the best competitor *primarily through people*. He knew the added benefits of being a public company would allow him to grow faster with ready funding reserves from affordable stock-offerings.

But what made Pulte Homes a strong competitor then, and now, is that Bill always realizes that he needs good people, who offer ingenuity and simple solutions, no matter the problem. People who persist, whose common sense matches their know-how. People who embrace change, but stay true to Pulte's core values. Who take risks, but understand the customer and the trade. Who are willing to learn, and courageous enough to tweak operational procedures to make everyday tasks simpler as the company grows more complex.

Neil Armstrong photographing the Appolo 11 spacecraft, July 20, 1969.
Photograph courtesy of NASA.

Building A Legacy

*"I never was afraid to take a calculated risk.
And I was never afraid to make changes."*

The right people, calculated risks, and educated changes – this is the Pulte competitive "trifecta." Like Bill's values, these philosophies weren't quickly chosen, but developed throughout Bill's boyhood. However, like the difficult-to-win yet high-yielding racing bet specifying the top three horses, Bill knew these three were exact, and inseparable. He knew these three were needed to come in first, second, *and* third.

Bill also learned early on, while playing *Monopoly* with his brother and sisters, that, if he were the first to buy the key properties, he would ultimately win the game. In the unforgiving world of production housing, Bill's competitive drive, however, showed itself not on *Monopoly's* Park Place, but the Bloomfield Hills' streets that led to his first Michigan subdivision, Concord Green.

With a miniscule promotional budget and a small militia of freshly painted green jalopies carrying signs advertising his new community, he boldly sputtered into other contractors' neighborhoods.

"He'd take a car to his competitors' models, who had money to advertise," says a Pulte Homes executive. "He would park at the curb. He knew the city ordinances, that you could leave a car, as long as it was licensed, on the curb, providing it was moved every 24 hours.

"Parking enforcement would come by with a little chalk marker and mark the wheel," the executive says. "And that night, he would move the car up a couple of feet, so the person checking would see the tire had moved, a bit. It made competitors madder than heck.

"But there was nothing they could do."

Realizing: 'I Need Superstars'

Not long after the company went public in 1969, Pulte executives were invited to a Wall Street analysts' meeting.

Less than a dozen builders of that era, who leapt to public incorporation, were present. The analysts fired tough questions at the group. "I had my finance man with me because you know, I'm very good at arithmetic, but I'm not a financier," Bill says. "I had no idea what they were talking about: Price-to-earnings ratios, etcetera, etcetera."

When the conversation shifted, however, and they started discussing construction, it dawned on Bill that he was the only expert in the room. "I realized I was dumber than heck about finance, but that they were dumber than heck about home building," Bill says.

The flight home gave Bill time to think. He realized he was now in the "major leagues" of business and needed to hire big-league talent, especially in finance, to be a stout competitor.

"I gotta get superstars," he thought.

It was the beginning of a hiring philosophy that for years would help Bill draft successful company leaders so that he could be the visionary and rely on key people to fine-tune and execute his vision.

"There is no such thing as a self-made man," Bill says. "Ego has destroyed a lot of people and companies, and ego is often a cover-up for a lack of self-confidence. Humility is usually a sign of self-confidence. Humble leaders can accomplish more than egotistical leaders."

It wouldn't be long after going public, that Bill stepped into the chairman's role, giving up the CEO's seat, to now almost exclusively trust his leaders, managers, and front-line employees to take the company to the places he had mapped, first in his mind and then for all who followed him.

Early in Pulte Homes' history Bill was presented with an Award of Excellence at the National Association of Home Builders convention.

Bill knew his company's future would be borne on the strength of well-trained people, the right attitude, and specific skills. As years passed, he would never shy away from changing corporate structure or making bold personnel moves to ensure the integrity of his vision. He knew that by himself he couldn't achieve his goal to be the strongest competitor in the market.

"He needs smart people to drive things forward," says a Pulte Homes' board member. "In his opinion, he thinks most CEOs have surrounded themselves with people in the executive suite who are 'yes' men, not driving the company forward, but getting to a rung and holding on. That's not the case, never will be the case, at Pulte Homes. That's not the *Pulte Way*."

Always Do The Right Thing

In Minnesota, a major rainstorm caused a pond to overflow and flood the basements of a new Pulte community.

Although the drainage problem wasn't the company's fault, the Minnesota division repaired homes at a cost of $1.5 million. They prevented the problem from recurring by redesigning the downstream drainage pond in another community.

In Maryland, a customer selling his 10-year-old Pulte home called an inspector who discovered the kitchen overhang was deteriorated due to improperly installed flashing. While the home was long out of warranty, the Maryland division repaired it, because it had been built incorrectly.

Decisions, large and small, abide by a tone long established by Bill Pulte, for anyone in the company, as a true competitive advantage: Do the right thing.

"These are the types of decisions I expect you to be making in the field on a daily basis," Bill says. "Our core set of values doesn't leave any room for second guessing. We operate with honesty, integrity and trust, in everything we do.

"These values are uncompromising," Bill says.

"Our core set of values doesn't leave any room for second guessing. We operate with honesty, integrity, and trust, in everything we do."

> *"I believe we have the best people in America on our team and we have a great culture. It's a huge advantage we have over our competition."*

Five Talents To Compete

That philosophy, for Bill, gave rise to "Five Talents" – skills he believes every business needs to be a true competitor.

First, people must understand the trade – where to buy, how seasonal changes affect business, how to merchandise, what the customer wants, and the mechanics of construction itself.

Then comes business finance expertise – where does the money come from? How are people paid? What financial risks does the company face? "Most tradesmen have no idea, or don't want to get into the financial stuff," Bill says. "But, don't forget the craft of homebuilding. It should always guide the context of decisions. Don't let the accountants cut down on nails in the wall."

Leadership is the third talent. "The difference between a leader and a manager is a leader has vision," says Bill. "He knows where he wants to go, he doesn't necessarily know all the nitty-gritty to get there, but he sees the broad picture. He's not like a sergeant in the trenches: 'Take that hill, fellas.' No, he's willing to say: 'Come on fellas. Let's all take the hill.'"

Yet the ability to find and retain good managers – the fourth talent – is vitally important. Although a manager might not have the talent to create a vision, if you provide clear direction, he'll happily wade into the nitty-gritty and get you there. "And a good manager *will* get you there," Bill says.

The fifth talent, but by far the most important, is the talent to employ good people, the front line of the business. "Without good people, you can't do anything," Bill says. "You've gotta give good people the authority. You've gotta reward them financially. Don't look over their shoulders.

"Talk to Wall Street, the only person that's important is the shareholder," Bill says. "Talk to sales people, and customers are most important. Hogwash. The most important is *the employee*. If you've got happy employees, they will *make* the other two happy."

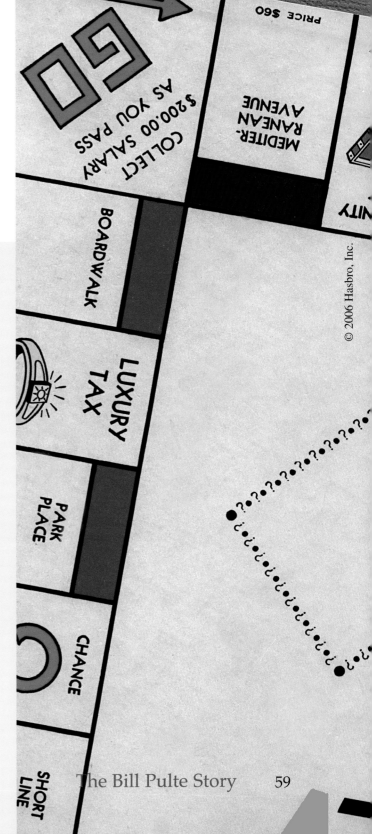

© 2006 Hasbro, Inc.

> ## "There may be somebody who's better at something than I am, but I'm not afraid to take them on."

Playing To Win: *Always* Climbing

Bill Pulte is known as a fierce competitor.

His sister Maureen says Bill's fighting spirit goes back to his boyhood. "On rainy days, we used to play *Monopoly* at a neighbor's screened-in porch. I loved it because you could hear the rain. … Bill always somehow ended up with Boardwalk, Park Place, the railroads – the most expensive places to land on. The rest of us couldn't afford his rent so we would eventually go broke."

"He likes to win, no question about that," says Karen Pulte. "We had some friends here at the lake on vacation and he got out a croquet set – these were three teenage boys – and they played all week, and he was always trying to beat them. The boys would laugh, until they caught on to the game and then they could imitate Bill to a T."

Golf also brings out Bill's competitiveness, especially when he's up against friend and regular partner, Pat Costello. "They have more games going on their scorecard than you could imagine," says Karen. "I would say, 'How do you know what you're shooting?' They would play Wolfman, C.O.D., carryovers, skins – all on the same card. They each play two balls."

"There may be somebody who's better at something than I am," says Bill, "but I'm not afraid to take them on."

At a company get-together, an imitation rock wall drew would-be climbers, and Bill wasn't deterred – he climbed the wall, too, attacking its most difficult approach.

When Bill looks into the mirror, the guy who looks back is 35, not 70-plus, says another executive. "It goes back to the simplicity by which Bill lives his life: 'The rock wall, everyone else is climbing it? Hey, I'm climbing it, too.'"

Wowing The Customer

In all aspects of the business, working with his leaders, Bill began to focus not just on quality construction but also on quality people, quality training, and ultimately quality service. He saw customer service, early on – just as Kennedy gazed at the moon – as the radiant future.

The type of ingenuity it took to sell Concord Green, coupled with persistence, market knowledge, and the relentless need to guarantee that competitors could do nothing to stop Pulte Homes, drove the success of hundreds of communities that followed.

"Our reasons for success haven't changed," says a company executive. "The changes we make and the risks we take today are no different than the changes Bill made and risks he took in the early days except, of course, the scale is much bigger."

Bill realized he must not just satisfy, but delight or "wow" customers. The only way to create that delight was through his employees, through proper training and a solid company culture.

To grow competitive muscle, Bill tapped this expertise through acquisitions, bringing on leaders, and later, developing leaders from within. He taught his leaders to accommodate change by constantly re-arranging the "sandboxes," and inspired them to increase customer delight through simple solutions.

To increase that delight, Bill wanted control of as many elements of the home-buying transaction as he could. Control meant owning the relationship with the buyer, and engendering loyalty.

One step in this direction was when Pulte formed a wholly-owned mortgage subsidiary in 1972. Bill was among the first home builders to take this step. His philosophy was as Pulte sold more homes, he wanted to make sure mortgages were processed swiftly and efficiently, so as not to delay closings. He also wanted to ensure the mortgage process didn't interfere with homes being delivered on time.

For an outside mortgage company, not much was at stake if a mortgage was delayed. But if a Pulte home was finished on the 15th of the month, Bill wanted to close on that home on the 16th, not the 30th.

The chairman's idea was invested around the concept of speeding the process – again a win-win for both the customer and the company. It was about speed and when a home was delivered. The fundamental goal was to make business easier and better, and to give Pulte a competitive boost.

At his core, Bill is a production home builder, and critical to that mindset is a good, solid construction schedule. No matter the changes Pulte made, Bill always wanted to keep in mind the appropriateness of managing to the production schedule. This is especially important in a company where the construction rate is faster than the national average and where executives always weigh vendors' efficient product delivery into production schedules.

In product design, Bill got architects to understand that "if momma ain't happy, nobody's happy," meaning: Designers, don't forget to look for the competitive edge lodged inside the home. Understand what the lady of the household wants. What's important to her?

Bill never forgets the customer.

For as long as many Pulte Homes' employees remember, Bill talked about putting kitchens adjacent to the garage so that groceries didn't have to be lugged across the house. Times have changed, but Bill continues to help the company keep up with features that meet the needs of the modern family. He has helped Pulte distinguish itself from builders who designed floor plans and didn't think them through, or see how a home worked from the homeowners' perspective.

In community design, Bill learned, and now teaches young leaders, how to design large communities. He explains how to make the most of land, and to provide what community residents really want in their community centers, so solutions aren't over-engineered or provide more than what the community needs, or can afford.

Educated changes like these – all keeping the customer in mind – only make Pulte Homes a stronger competitor.

"That's what helped our customer satisfaction scores go through the roof. Because we have a whole different sandbox in which we're playing the game."

Can-Do Spirit: 4-Day Frame-Out

Part of Bill Pulte's competitive fervor comes from his innate sense that no one can tell him "winning" is impossible.

In the early sixties, his sixth child just born, Bill faced one of his usual personal dilemmas for housing: *Where do I put all these kids?*

The effort that followed rivaled a modern-day *Extreme Makeover: Home Edition.* Bill bought an existing home that was too small, and because of an accelerated closing schedule, needed to move from his old house. So he designed an addition for his new place — overnight, almost. He organized a crew to work a long holiday weekend.

Joe Baranska, Bill's friend and one-time sales and marketing VP, remembers that the house had a tenant, who planned a weekend getaway. So Bill asked: *"Do you mind if I come and do a little work while you're gone?"*

The tenant's "OK" unleashed Bill's robust motivation.

The foundation people came. The carpenters came. The drywall people came. The painters came. "We watched them all coming down the street," says Joe.

When the tenant returned from his July 4 getaway, the two-story addition was framed, roofed and sheathed. Inside, a bathroom, bedrooms, and a family room were taking shape.

"Incredible," says Baranska.

"On Saturday and Sunday, people had a picnic across the street and the neighbors came to watch," Bill says. "I had guys on the roof. I had bricklayers. I had plumbers. I had electricians. … Forty guys on a little job, you need some coordination."

Human motivation and the daring to push the limits of what's humanly possible form the backbone of Bill's unrelenting spirit.

Rocketing To Success

To keep a competitive edge, Bill always drives at the simplicity of the solution. Bill's vision is to explore ways for the company to make and supply materials to its communities and perhaps eventually to those of other builders. His vision is working toward shaking up the supply chain dynamic, making Pulte Homes the most efficient builder in the country.

Through his own innovative solutions and patents, Bill has fostered a climate of ingenuity. Pulte Homes' ingenuity and technology cover many areas, but one example is a software system that helps sales offices better communicate and automatically update changes in platting information, plan selection, design, options, mortgages, and contracts – another effort to maintain the lead on competitors.

As he launched Pulte forward with his innovations, Bill continued to work simultaneously toward geographic and product line diversification.

Pulte's foray into Washington, D.C. in 1963 taught Bill how important geographic diversification was in the formation of a competitive and healthy corporation.

"Our geographic footprint is a tremendous competitive advantage, because we are one of the few major builders that are in virtually every major city," says Bill. "This allows us to tap into the hot markets, and ride out those that may be going through some economic downturns."

In 1970, by buying American Builders, which had been selling to home buyers via Federal Housing Administration and Veterans Affairs loans, Pulte made its first attempt at a lower-priced house, and therefore, product diversification.

Then came the oil crisis and the rust-belt recession – idling factories from Pennsylvania west to Minnesota.

"I think we built 800 houses in Detroit in 1979," Bill says. "And in 1981, we did 75. But in 1981 or 1982, we built 3,000 homes in Denver and two years prior, only 250." The balance that came from geographic and product diversification made Pulte a powerful competitor.

"Our geographic footprint is a tremendous competitive advantage, because we are one of the few major builders that are in virtually every major city."

Pulte's relationships with customers, assessed through rigorous annual surveys, earn it J.D. Power awards year after year.

Bill's calculated risks and educated changes rocketed the company to success. Bringing on so many new employees in the 1980s to put out 10,000 complex products each year sparked a need for world-class training, particularly in quality production and service, which would become integral parts of the Pulte culture.

In answer to and in anticipation of challenges like those, Bill launched Pulte University in 1980. It was among the industry's first production training programs. Later, he endorsed the Pulte Quality Leadership Program to train promising future executives to better understand Pulte's home-building philosophy, and customer-focused mindset.

Pulte University was the predecessor to Top Gun mentoring, Emerging Leaders, Foundations of Management, Building Quality Relationships, and other employee development programs. Pulte University focused on construction and land, its rigid black books teaching how to do appropriate take-offs, costing, and construction. In fact, the importance and value of these historical training methods grew as Pulte grew, and continue to be a critical factor in the company's ongoing success.

Customer Delight

More often than not, solutions that ratchet up the competitive edge require a different perspective.

One example that deeply affected both the corporate culture and how home buyers viewed Pulte Homes, while at the same time creating a distinct competitive advantage, was the change in how management looked at warranty service. Rather than simply focusing on fixing problems, Bill's constant emphasis is on delighting the customer. This has been integrated as one of the company's primary values.

In the late 1990s, a shift was made to hire superintendents with superb interpersonal skills. They were trained for six weeks in communications, putting the customer first, and understanding the customer's unique needs. This training caused a large shift in customer satisfaction scores – but it wasn't enough.

> *"So many times over the years I have changed the rules of the sandbox. Never be afraid to make changes."*

Bill encouraged his leaders to hire executives from other customer-focused industries. Their ideas helped transform the warranty department into the customer relations department, whose primary objective was to ensure that the customers were *delighted* with their experience of buying a home from Pulte.

This was accomplished through the newly named customer relations department deciding its people would manage the home-buying experience from start to finish. And the department put a non-traditional expert in the job. A personable, well-trained individual was focused primarily on relationships, even more than on house construction details. This new person told customers: "Every time you have a problem, call me. I'll get the answer."

"That's what helped our customer satisfaction scores go through the roof," says Bill. "Because we have a whole different sandbox in which we're playing the game."

And man, the sand was flying.

No Cash, No Pants

Bill always has done a lot with a little, almost as if to test the dimension of human possibility, to test human ingenuity under competition-like conditions.

He walks around with little or no cash. He constantly tests the limits of his car's gas tank. He travels as light as a monk. He'll typically show up at the airport for a two-day trip with one small carry-on – containing a change of underwear, socks and a shirt. "What else do I need?" Bill asks the unbeliever.

His wife, Karen, always tries to sneak an extra sweater into his bag. "I don't need it," he protests. "He's a minimalist," Karen explains.

When Pulte Homes went public, Stock Exchange officials wanted Bill to come to Wall Street to ring the opening bell.

Stepping out of a cab from LaGuardia Airport at the Exchange, wearing his one suit, Bill reached his leg to the curb. His pants split.

Nonplussed, he walked into the Exchange and politely asked the front-desk receptionist: "Do you have stapler?" With a 'be right back,' he zipped to the men's room, removed the pants, stapled the seam of the ripped trousers, and carefully slipped them back on.

As Bill rang the bell that day, only he knew a handful of staples stood between him and a much more open policy of corporate introduction.

"I walked into the men's room in Washington National Airport one time and he's sitting there getting his shoes shined," says Joe Baranska. "And he says, 'Thank God somebody walked in who I know.' He didn't know I was in town. I didn't know he was in town. He says, 'I haven't got enough money to pay this guy.'

"Well, the funny thing about it," says Joe, "is I didn't have any money either. And a guy named Harvey Pinski, a cabinet guy, walks in right then, and we said, 'Oh, my gosh, you just bailed us both out.'"

Bill Pulte: Always pushing the envelope ... *and stapling it when it rips.*

Bill, Finally Going To College

Bill says Pulte has proven that when you hire people for personal attributes and their aptitude for learning, they're more successful in the long run than those hired simply with the right skills.

While Pulte finds some employees with the attitude and aptitude it seeks in the industry, by looking outside, and to college campuses, Pulte finds a larger pool of candidates. "If we recruit the right ones, they are bright and willing learners," Bill says. "We can hire them for the attributes that we know will fit into our culture, then train them on the technical skills. This source of talent will truly be our competitive edge."

It is not uncommon for Pulte Homes to hire hundreds of college graduates each year; the company's next closest competitor hires less than a quarter of that number. These will be the people who drive the future customer delight.

"Our future depends on us getting the right people in at entry level, to help us run the company long-term," Bill says.

For employees already on board, Bill sees personal growth as key to the future. Not only is this good for people, it's critical for success. "Our employees are the ones who have helped us grow," Bill says. By sending people to Top Gun, or taking days off to attend management development classes, or getting the team out of the field for a morning of learning and exchanging ideas, the company embraces the view that training and development reaps enormous dividends.

If people are well-trained and well-rewarded, they'll be happy to make customer delight Pulte's competitive advantage, Bill says. And Pulte Homes knows that understanding the customer is the competitive advantage.

Simplification & Segmentation

The drive toward operational excellence took a step forward when Pulte acquired DiVosta Homes in 1998. The DiVosta acquisition made Bill further recognize the beauty of simplification, an initiative that consumes him, and the company, to this day.

DiVosta built a tremendous brand following by offering great quality and unmatched value, utilizing simplified options and fewer upgrades. The approach allows DiVosta to build a house in 47 days, far less than the industry average, and offer more house for the money.

Building a house requires hundreds of contractors assembling thousands of parts for a product where no two are the same. By simplifying business products and processes, Bill realizes the company has the potential to reduce construction costs, improve construction cycle time, and increase quality. If today Pulte orders thousands of window types from 15 manufacturers, how much more efficient would the company be if it only ordered a few types from the two best manufacturers? Using simplification initiatives, Bill knows Pulte could drive total costs down by hundreds of millions of dollars each year.

It was not long ago that Pulte had thousands of floor plans, in more than 600 communities. But, by creating a library of the best-selling plans, the number of plans has been reduced by about half, with another reduction under consideration.

By focusing on fewer floor plans and options, Pulte Homes will not only deliver greater value to the customer, but also make the process of selection easier. Through understanding what options people truly value and making those options standard, Pulte is able to create the win-win relationships with customers that has earned it so many J.D. Power awards.

Besides understanding the considerable benefits of simplification for both the customer and the company, Bill was always very good at finding out where customers wanted to live. The map of West Bloomfield and Bloomfield Townships he colored marked the parks, neighborhoods, and commercial properties so he knew where the empty parcels of land were located.

Understanding that different types of customers would buy in different neighborhoods helped the company develop the mindset to understand customers and where they wanted to live based on their housing needs.

The concept of target consumer groups, or TCGs, developed from that idea. By segmenting, and organizing consumers into groups that act similarly, Pulte recognizes that different groups have different needs and there are different ways to reach them.

It sounds simple, but it's revolutionary for the building industry, and segmentation by TCG means business opportunity is no longer a guessing game.

Customer groups that are underserved can be identified by comparing the supply of homes and lots with the demand of each consumer group. By knowing where people want to live and what "products" they want to live in, Pulte can tailor offerings to meet their needs.

"Bill has always had a plan," says a company executive. "And his plan today is don't just do things, think them through."

In his drive to be the best competitor, Bill taps common-sense thinking to get people to understand the difference … *the Pulte difference.*

Spreading The Webb

In acquisitions, Bill has taken a competitor's calculated risks. "Bill is not afraid to pull the trigger," says a Pulte board member.

A giant leap for Pulte, reminiscent of the leap to go public in 1969, was the $1.7 billion merger with Del Webb Corporation in 2001 – a bold stroke to change the face of Pulte Homes. At the time it was the largest merger in housing industry history.

Del Webb's unmatched position among active adult buyers, strong brand names, land pipeline, and more than 7,000 annual closings helped Pulte gain a dominant position with the country's fastest growing demographic – people age 55 and older. The merger made the company the nation's largest homebuilder.

But behind the scenes of the largest industry merger ever, was the fact that it could have fallen apart. Bill was insistent on quickly integrating the two companies' cultures.

Bill wanted to make certain that through the process, the Pulte culture would prevail. There were times when executives weren't sure the deal would make it, but Bill remained serene and composed, insistent that there would be a way to make it work.

A Pulte home in Argentina.

Each Decade, A Vault Of Knowledge

Bill has said his mistakes always made him a better competitor.

In the 1970s, he learned two things – that he should have entered the Houston market before Atlanta to take advantage of the Texas oil boom, and that building contemporary homes in Michigan required better research.

While Bill loves contemporary architecture, he learned the hard way that less than 3% of people feel the same way. Most like more traditional homes. "Don't build what you like personally – build what the customer wants," says an executive of Bill's lesson from that decision.

Business overseas hasn't been without lessons, either.

The pull-out from Argentina was predicated on not having a full understanding of how a foreign country operates when facing hyper-inflation, and what it means when a foreign currency devalues to the point that an investment's worth is cut in half.

But to Bill, these things were time lost and distractions. No lesson went unlearned, not for this competitor, always willing to shoulder risk, and vault over the competition.

The irony of the Argentinian experience is that the name Pulte lives on in that country. So impressed were local builders with Pulte's approach to quality housing that many now advertise their homes as *Casa de Pulte*.

"He is the calm in the storm," says an executive. "Talk to people and you will find Bill Pulte is the calm in *any* storm."

Del Webb spent four decades building active adult communities, catering to the 55-and-older set. But, in addition to propelling Pulte Homes into the active adult community market all over the country, the acquisition made Pulte more diversified – a key to the company's success.

With Baby Boomers approaching retirement, the nation's 65-and-over population could increase nearly 80 percent by 2025, according to U.S. Census Bureau estimates. And those aged 55 and older number 63 million – that's set to grow to 80 million or more. By 2045, the number could break 120 million, which would represent 30% of the projected U.S. population.

Del Webb's active adult communities were primarily in the Southwest. But research shows that more than half the people surveyed retire within 100 miles, or three hours from where they grew up.

For Pulte, that meant building Del Webb communities in existing Pulte markets, in Michigan, Massachusetts, and New Jersey, among others. Now, still in the role of visionary, Bill encourages Active Adult executives to develop standard amenity packages to leverage existing, proven designs.

Today, roughly a third of Pulte's overall investment is targeted toward the active adult segment.

But, Pulte isn't betting future growth on any single demographic. The company is known as one of the most diverse builders, in nearly every geographic market, with homes at all price points. The Homeowner for Life program strengthens brand loyalty, drawing customers from one Pulte home to another as they step from one phase of their lives into the next.

Not a bad place to be as a competitor – no, *the* competitor.

Look To What Is Possible

So how does Pulte Homes continue to be the best, to shoot for the moon?

Bill reminds everyone at Pulte to stop using the competition as a yardstick. Stop thinking about one or two main consumer groups. "We must stop operating only where we are comfortable," he says. "Change."

He envisions, as the leading competitor, building 200,000 homes, showing Wall Street a 20% market share, and $75 billion in revenue. Controlling the best land. Offering loans approved online within five minutes or less. Logging a mortgage capture rate of 100%.

In his mind, that's only years away. Look beyond the building industry, he says.

Auto companies can tell us something about delivering a completed product, by how few times they miss "major items" on delivery. "Would you accept even one major item problem in an automobile?" Bill asks.

It's ironic, in a way, that J.D. Power and Associates, long known for its consumer satisfaction and product quality work in the automotive industry, in recent years expanded to serve other industries, including home building. Because now Bill, who always turns to the auto industry for examples or history, whether of success or failure, has another connection to cars, as Pulte wins one J.D. Power award after another.

"*Forget about how things* have been done. *Look to* what is possible."

"We always need to be on the lookout for ways to improve and challenge the status quo," the chairman says. "We've got to stop being burdened by the past. Forget about how things *have been done*. Look to *what is possible*."

Pulte Homes now has distinct advantages over the competition in money, expertise, brands, vision, and a desire to make it happen. In 2002, *Money* magazine listed Pulte Homes as a "30-Year Super Stock," and *BusinessWeek* twice named Pulte among the "Top 50 Best Performing Companies."

Bill's efforts to keep Pulte focused on quality and service contributed to J.D. Power naming the company the inaugural recipient of its Platinum Award for customer satisfaction among America's largest home building companies.

All because Bill hired the right people, took calculated risks, and made educated changes. Bill stayed true to his core values.

"We stand for quality and our ongoing relationship with the customer will continue to delight our home buyers," the chairman says. "And that will be our competitive advantage."

With focus, and through people, a mission is being fulfilled.

But now, Bill guides us to what is beyond. Like Bill, we will not need so much to think of where we've been.

We need to think of where we'll go.

The Competitor
in full swing.

Chapter Four
The Whiz Kid

Not long after Bill Gates and Paul Allen huddled in a Harvard dorm room debugging code for the first home computer, Bill Pulte was in his garage cutting, nailing, wiring, and drywalling prototypes of another sort.

It was there that Bill, normally collaborative, let the solitary Whiz Kid in him play. It was the early 1980s, and his sons and daughters were in their teenage years and older. So it was a time when Bill could more easily tap the component of his nature that creates, apart from others and alone. The work fueled his whirring mind.

"I remember him coming home in his Mustang, and the car would be weighed down with sinks, toilets, faucets, 2x4s, electrical wire," recalls one of his sons.

Bill's prototypes were the framework for his "Dream Plant," which grew out of a modest first effort established in a one-time Wyoming fertilizer warehouse. The plant gave birth to Bill's belief that house parts – walls, decks, web trusses, sub-floors, roofs, even standard-sized bathrooms – could be put together like car parts, in a factory, with high quality, and shipped to the site where they'd be assembled efficiently and cost-effectively. The resulting home would be stronger, longer-lasting, and more energy efficient than stick-built houses.

Pre-fabricated wall assemblies roll off the production line at Bill's first plant in Wyoming.

"Everybody thinks that if it's handmade, it's better. But handmade is not always better. In fact, I wouldn't want a handmade car today, or a toaster."

"He'd build the prototype of a bath in his garage, ship it to the plant, and we'd use it as a production model to make our production decisions," says a Pulte executive.

"Month after month, I would help him build all these things," says Bill's son. "And then, after seeing the factory in the early 1980s, I suddenly knew why he was doing all this stuff."

"If we build 100,000 houses someday, we have to do it the same way they build cars," Bill would say. "Every dashboard is the same. Maybe a different color. It's either a Cadillac, or a Chevrolet, or an Oldsmobile. But the dials are all the same."

That's a Big Picture Thinker.

A Restless Mind

Bill Pulte, like the automotive icons who preceded his generation, has been a Big Picture Thinker since the days when his parents couldn't understand how he possibly could knit together a house at age 18. A boyhood friend says Bill's mother used to go to church just to pray her son wouldn't go broke.

Bill didn't stop with his first patent, No. 4,015,385, filed June 2, 1974 and approved April 5, 1977, for the House With Unfinished Bonus Space. No, he has that same mindset today. Bill still thinks like a craftsman. While his big-picture solutions have evolved from when he was a tradesman-builder, to custom builder, to production builder, what keeps him vibrant now is his tinkering nature.

It's his long-term view that a house can always be built better, and in ways unimagined using today's economic models and methods. Besides dreaming up better systems to create quality and energy efficiencies, he continues to improve house performance from a builder's perspective, while planning for the reality of a decreasing skilled labor pool and increasing the quality of home products.

Bill knows it won't be easy, but he'll never be satisfied, so he tinkers with concepts and ideas. His obsession these days is his teenage passion: Having fun with homes.

"I love to create new ideas," he says. "Whether it's the whole plan or whether it's just a part of a plan. I've always liked to create."

While Pulte Home Sciences wouldn't officially be formed until 1999, its goal was always in Bill's mind: Build better houses and better construction processes. "Better and faster" motivates and inspires any Whiz Kid or Big Picture Thinker. Bill Pulte has a half-dozen patents, pending patents, or approvals for patents to vouch for his restless mind.

What no one can know are the number of existing patents for products that Bill and Pulte Homes Sciences engineers helped their suppliers and vendors improve or create. These are designs that he and his team directly influenced, yet never benefited from financially. They include the baffle-and-dam venting system for airflow in insulated attics that is used almost universally in new homes today, and the steel floor that Dietrich Industries markets as the "TradeReady Floor."

"I love to create new ideas. Whether it's the whole plan or whether it's just a part of a plan. I've always liked to create."

Perhaps Bill's ideas were doodled on ice cream napkins. OK, maybe that's a stretch, but like the cool appeal of an ice cream cone on a hot summer day, Bill's best ideas have stood the test of time.

"Bill's an ideas guy," says a Pulte executive. "He knows that 90% of ideas don't work. But the 10% that make it? Boy, those could change the way everyone looks at how things gets done."

Telescopic Genius

If you asked Bill, he'd say: "I never invented much." Yet, he always has been ahead of his time. His humble assessment doesn't capture how he lives now, as a Whiz Kid with his thoughts whirring. Bits and pieces of exterior finishing trim, ridge caps, or roof samples in his happily chaotic office are the only hints of what he envisions the future might bring.

What others can't see might lead to even greater discoveries – snap-in trim that needs no nails, or extremely lightweight composite roofs that draw on aerospace technology. Imagine a roof so light it could be set in place in one piece, yet be so tough that it lasts 100 years.

Such are the far-reaching thoughts of the Whiz Kid.

Bill has the ability to look at the horizon and visualize what it means, counting every tree, rock, and feature as if looking through a telescopic lens, not missing anything. Bill can move the lens in and out, moving with great ease from the details to the big picture. "That's his genius," says a Pulte executive. "He is clearly getting sharper and more creative as he's getting older."

Bill won't be deterred from his vision and ambition when it comes to his belief that investments in housing construction research and development should be treated just like pharmaceutical and healthcare R&D, or R&D in any major industry. He believes that just as Pulte invests in land, it should invest in housing construction research.

Who, like Pulte, consistently invests in this type of research?

Who would think to use material, perfected for precisely molded car interior components, on houses, as incredibly durable trim?

The Whiz Kid.

"The idea of Pulte Home Sciences is to change the way America builds houses," Bill says. "We've been doing it one way for so many years. There must be better systems out there."

Pultrim, one of Bill's inventions, is a preformed, low-maintenance trim that lasts longer than other trim products. It draws on aerospace and automotive technology.

Salve For An Inventive Mind

Somewhere, in one of Bill's bureaus or desk drawers, sits an envelope that has never been opened.

Inside is a hand-drawn diagram and a description of a device that might change the world – or at least help squeeze the most from a toothpaste tube.

One of Bill's sons recalls the day his father showed him the unopened envelope he said he had mailed to himself, back in the 1960s. "He came up with an idea similar to the SPAM lid. The can has a key that inserts into a metal flap and the key peels off the lid. He had the same concept for a toothpaste tube.

"The key is on the bottom of the tube, and as you push it up with your thumb and forefinger, everything left in the tube comes out so there's no waste inside."

But Bill's schematic and explanation still sits in the unopened letter. He told his son if anyone ever discovered the idea and filed a patent, he would open the envelope he mailed to himself, proving he thought of it first.

The genesis for this idea obviously was not construction, but witnessing 14 kids, squeezing the heck out of their toothpaste tubes.

Another case of Bill always pushing the envelope, or in this case, never opening it.

Bill pauses on a European trip to appreciate an innovative design.

Home Design Leader

Bill Pulte's patented invention of a "House With Unfinished Bonus Space" made the company a stronger competitor and the industry's design leader. It helped to reinvigorate the Michigan division, knocked flat by a decline in housing purchases prompted by the 1970s oil embargo crisis and skyrocketing mortgage interest rates. What the Bonus Space or Expandable House concept did was tap an unmet consumer need.

Not only did it allow home buyers to have a say in how space in their house would be finished and used, it provided growing families the opportunity to make those decisions later. In the meantime, the space didn't have to be heated or cooled; homeowners had the option to finish it themselves; and they could enjoy the satisfaction of knowing not much more had been paid for that future space.

It's not by chance the House With Unfinished Bonus Space is the only patent of several Bill holds that's framed on his office wall. It's both a symbol and the reality of the elegant simplicity of thinking Bill has always sought to infuse into Pulte Homes.

"Bill was always thinking how to grow, innovate, and move the residential construction business to a new form," says a Pulte executive. "If change wasn't happening, he would make it happen, to benefit the company and the consumer."

A Home Parade arranged by Joe Baranska in Michigan included the expandable house. It wasn't long before the home, described as "smart as a fox," was on TV, radio, in newspapers, and on CBS national news. Why was it "foxy?" It looked like a mansion outside, but had two unfinished rooms inside.

A 1970s marketing piece aimed at potential home buyers who wanted "big and beautiful" outside, with "room to grow" inside.

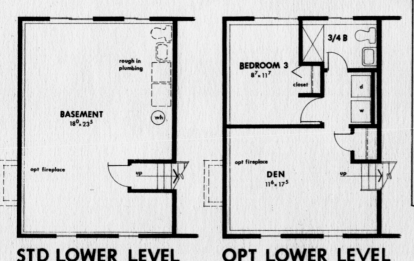

The lower level can be left unfinished, offering you special bonus space that you can plan to finish as your family's needs grow. You'll save $$$!

PULTE
Owner Built Homes

. . . or finish the lower level and feature a large recreation room, warmed by an inviting fireplace (optional). The fireplace in this recreation room is a welcomed bonus and helps to set the mood for family togetherness in fun and relaxation. The third bedroom is especially well suited for your growing teenager who appreciates his privacy. When he's off to college, convert the room into a study . . . a place for you to read, rest, and regroup or if you need, use the third bedroom as a workshop or hobby room. The Bridgeport . . . an excellent buy for the family on the grow!

BEDROOM 3
$8^7 \times 11^7$

3/4 B

closet

BASEMENT
$18^0 \times 23^5$

rough in plumbing

wh

opt fireplace

DEN
$11^6 \times 17^5$

opt fireplace

up

STD LOWER LEVEL
(floor dimensions approximate)

OPT LOWER LEVEL

Keys To Success

If inventors are prone to absent-mindedness, it is because their minds are usually full of more important thoughts.

Bill Pulte has always left his keys either on or under the front floor mat of his car wherever he goes, no matter where he goes, so as not to lose them. "And he never locks the car unless you ask, or if something is in it," says his wife, Karen.

But the story that takes the cake is the time he drove his cherry red Cadillac Eldorado to catch a flight out of Detroit's Metro Airport. As usual, Bill left the car unlocked, the keys under the mat.

When he returned from the trip, his car was gone. It had been impounded before when, running late and unable to find a parking spot, he had parked it illegally. Thinking this had happened again, he flagged down a security officer.

He learned his car had been stolen. Airport Police told him Wayne County Sheriff's officers discovered it with a broken side window and a hot-wired ignition ... the keys still under the driver's side mat.

The irony, perhaps, wasn't lost on Bill's whirring mind: Even obvious solutions go unnoticed, particularly to those intent on ordinary outcomes.

As with most innovations, it started with perspiration. Joe remembers Bill inviting him and Dave Kellett over to his office. The brainstorming resulted in a challenge for Bill: Come up with a home that offered more for the money and looked more expensive than it really cost.

Bubbling up from Bill's restless mind, using his common sense, was the idea of unfinished space intended as a family room or for other purposes. For buyers, this practical and cost-saving solution created an emotional response and they flocked to it.

"The house looked like a mansion because of the pillars across the front," Joe says. It had a side-loading garage so the front elevation was uninterrupted, contributing to a stylish colonnade look. It was about 2,100 square-feet inside but, from the outside, it looked at least 1,000 square-feet larger.

As potential buyers walked through the model, Bill and his sales crew listened. As she saw the unfinished space, one woman commented, "What a wonderful place for the ballet studio." A man observed, "Wow, I can put my model trains up here."

Bill asked designers to draw large renderings illustrating ways the rooms could be used: A family room, a ballet studio, a model train room, a game room – about a half-dozen pictures in all. He hung these renderings from the ceiling in the Bonus Space.

The Bonus Space saved home buyers $10,000 of what it would cost, at the time, to finish the room. In today's terms, that would have been about $50,000. So while the space saved the buyer thousands of dollars, it gave families options beyond just a newer, larger home with space they needed. It anticipated the remodeling trend that would take shape in the mid-1980s and explode in the 1990s.

But in the 1970s, the appeal was more emotional: Looks big and beautiful outside. Room to grow inside. It further advanced the company slogan: "Pulte offers the most square footage for the money."

"The newspapers ate this up," Joe says. "This was the most innovative concept that had come along in years, the expandable house. The houses sold like hotcakes in a very tough market."

Sunday, March 4, 1979

Expandable house expanded horizons for Pulte Homes

By JACK WOERPEL
News Staff Writer

Bill Pulte built his first house when he was 18 years old, fresh out of high school. He sold the four-room bungalow for $10,000. That was 28 years ago.

Last year his firm built nearly 4,000 houses and sold them for $205 million. It has about 6,000 acres of land under development, including about 1,000 acres in Michigan.

Pulte Home Corp. has 11 divisions operating in Michigan, Maryland, Virginia, Pennsylvania, Indiana, Illinois, Wyoming, Colorado,

> **'Basically, the idea is to sell for $32,000 a house that has the look from the curb of a $100,000 house. The extra two large rooms are unfinished.'**

Arizona, Georgia, Texas and Puerto Rico.

"We plan to start operations in Seattle this year," Pulte said during a conversaion in his West Bloomfield Township office. "We will probably set up in one other state this year, too, but I'm not ready to talk about it."

One important element in Pulte's success has been his patented design for an expandable house. By tucking the garage into the house structure instead of tacking it on at one side or in front, he makes the house seem much larger than conventional homes of the same square footage.

THE COMPANY has had its share of controversy, as have most large production builders. Some of his home buyers in Farmington Hills picketed in his subdivision last spring because they said their houses were not being completed on time.

But Pulte says the delays were caused by the weather and by road bans which kept ready-mix trucks from delivering concrete to the site. People who were already in their houses were unhappy about wading through mud. And people who could not yet move into their houses because they weren't finished were unhappy because they were afraid their favorable mortgage commitments would expire.

"But as soon as the road bans were off and we could get in there, we got the driveways and walks in and finished the jobs," said Ronald G. Smith, the president of the Michigan division. "The television crew which had filmed the original picketing came back out to show the finished houses. But instead of pointing out that we had finished up as quickly as we could, they claimed credit for 'forcing' us to do right by the customers.

"We wanted to finish those houses just as much as the people wanted them finished," Smith said.

PULTE CONTROLS the far-flung operations of his company, but he is neither president nor chairman of the board. His title now is chairman of the executive committee. The president of Pulte Home Corp. is C. Howard Johnson. The chairman of the board of directors is James Grosfeld.

Pulte was just another Detroit builder until 1963, when he happened to see an article in a building magazine about the houses being built in the Washington area by the Kettler Brothers Co. "Those houses looked a lot like the ones I was building in the suburbs of Detroit. They were selling very well in the hot Washington market. I figured I could do as well as Kettler in Washington, so I started operations there. We've been doing fine there ever since.

"And that got us started in other

Pulte's trademark is a big-looking house, with the garage tucked inside.

parts of the country. In two of our divisions, Colorado and Puerto Rico, we bought small companies and used them as a nucleus for growth. In Texas and Arizona we bought the land and other assets of small builders, then hired those builders as our general managers.

"But mostly we just move some of our staff out there and start an operation," he said.

PULTE BELIEVES the building business has more opportunities for young people than most of the professions. "I think a young man can make more money in the home building business than in law or medicine, if he just goes at it right," Pulte said. Ronald G. Smith started a few years ago as a salesman in Pulte's Denver subdivision. Now he is president of Pulte Homes of Michigan, Inc.

"Our project managers, who are responsible for construction and sales of several hundred houses, are responsible for construction and sales of several hundred houses and make from $50,000 to $125,000 a year, with profit sharing. Our division managers make a lot more than that," he said.

"But no colleges are really

training construction superintendents or sales managers or mortgage specialists," he said. "We hire college graduates and have to teach them how to get the most from materials."

Old-time Detroit area carpenters and other building tradesmen are "the best you'll find anywhere in the country," Pulte said. "The unions really used to do a good job training apprentices. But a lot of the new men are a different matter. They don't have the skills.

"EVEN SO, the Detroit carpenters are better than the trades we are finding in other parts of the country. In Laramie, Wyoming, we have built a plant to produce panelized walls up to 44 feet long — because the carpenters there aren't skilled enough to produce the walls on site as efficiently as we require.

"We are going to build such a plant in Michigan within the next few years, a more sophisticated version which will do more of the work. Part of the reason is that in such a plant we can work right through the weather and can control the quality better than on the site.

Continued on Page

Pulte's Expandable House is featured in *The Detroit News*.

One Home, Delivered, In 360 Minutes

The same kind of innovative, gutsy thinking led to Bill's Dream Plant in Laramie, Wyoming. Why Laramie?

Business was booming in the west and there were no established builders, supply lines, or trade base in this area of the country. Route 80 provided a direct route to many markets. The city offered businesses tax-free bonds to create jobs and the University of Wyoming was a ready source of affordable, skilled and unskilled employees. All that, coupled with a short construction season, made Wyoming the perfect location for factory built homes.

Bill had hired a general contractor, a former general manager of a lumberyard that operated a truss and wall panel division, to start up the first 30,000-square-foot plant in an old fertilizer warehouse.

By the time Pulte employees at that plant were building 800 homes a year, Bill understood what their factory methods could accomplish, and he visited Japan to study manufacturing methods there. At the time, visitors could get into Japanese factories without signing non-compete disclosures. Bill studied the factories and came back loaded with ideas.

Bill's second plant in Wyoming:
The "Dream Plant."

After his overseas journeys, Bill designed the layout and tooling for the Dream Plant, in a new 122,000-square-foot building. It was then that he started shipping to the plant the bathroom and kitchen mock-ups he made in his garage. "That's where Bill started getting his juices flowing," says a Pulte executive. "He tapped into his creativity, truly industrializing this effort."

In 1983 at the peak of its production, the 120 employees at the Wyoming Dream Plant produced 1,500 homes a year, about four per day over three shifts. The homes were shipped throughout Wyoming and to Denver, where oil drilling companies were based in the 1980s.

The packages included floor and roof trusses. Wall panels were built with siding, windows, and exterior trim installed. Interior packages included cabinets, doors, interior trim, and carpeting. Some homes were even painted in the factory. They were assembled in the field from paneled pieces, and the finished materials were shipped separately, after the drywall was installed.

As Bill became more of an industrialist, he said he wanted to make more parts, like bathrooms and kitchens, instead of loose cabinets. He wanted to do more pre-assembled work. "He'd do these mock-ups and we'd ship them as finished kits," says a Pulte executive.

The Dream Plant also fueled the start of "Pulte Owner-Built Homes," a "beat inflation" plan for the times that delivered a "scattered site" home package to the owner's lot, or to builders not aligned with the company. The factory shipped packages all along the front range of the Rocky Mountains.

The energy boom peaked in Wyoming and Colorado, and demand dried up. The sales volume evaporated in the west and it was too costly to ship products east or south, so the plant no longer made sense financially. The day of the Pulte factory built home was over … for the time being.

Bill shuttered the plant in November 1985, but was comforted by the realization that he, and the company, had learned more than anyone would have dreamed possible. He would revive the idea of component building in factories many years later.

"We've been building houses one way for so many years. There must be better systems out there."

Pulte Construction

Your Pulte home package arrives with a full Pulte construction crew. Pulte's experienced construction team unloads and erects your Home Package in a few days you own a locked structure complete with exterior walls, exterior doors, windows, sheathing, siding, and all interior walls, interior floors, stairways, and a weather-resistant truss constructed roof! No worries about lumber unloading and pilferage before its installed.

Phone or visit Pulte today to discover the additional benefits of the "Owner Built" Program including . . .

★ **Triple-paned** wood framed sliding glass doors and windows (including removable storm unit) . . . standard in every home we offer.

★ Innovative financing programs for qualified buyers . . . including the new **"no points"** financing plan (subject to availability).

★ Pulte's **Value Analysis** . . . prove for yourself that Pulte's Owner Built Program is the best value for you.

An early Pulte marketing piece demonstrates Bill's innovative approach to home building.

Handmade Toasters And Nuclear Submarines

Working directly with manufacturers and the trades, Bill wanted to tinker with problems of distribution, improving how goods are delivered to, and purchased for, the home. Why should a builder have to rely on vendors for solutions? Why couldn't builders explore, invent, make, distribute, maybe even franchise, those products themselves? Why couldn't a builder have product distribution centers?

Bill wanted to "value engineer" a home, asking, for example: How do you continue to improve the quality of a house but, perhaps, use one less truss or fewer shingles? Value engineering meant considering moving a bathroom from one side of a bedroom to another, so plumbing runs were shorter, cutting costs. Ever the Whiz Kid, for years he constantly imagined how to do things differently than they'd been done before.

Bill always sought to change how Pulte homes were built, and explored strategies in advanced homebuilding called "component manufacturing," a process proven in everything from automobiles to nuclear submarines.

Pulte Home Sciences developed proven methods to manufacture concrete foundation panels, deck panels, structurally insulated wall panels (SIPs), steel interior walls, and Bill's latest invention for fascia, soffit, gutter and frieze molding: Pultrim, whose patent is pending.

"Anytime you want to change, you've got to change the mentality to go with it."

"Everybody thinks that if it is handmade, it is better," the chairman says. "It might be – if it's built by a good craftsman. But handmade is not always better. In fact, I wouldn't want a handmade car today. I wouldn't want a handmade toaster.

"The SIP wall is, by far, a better wall than the standard 2x4 wall," he says. "Steel studs make a better wall, by far, than 2x4s. Factory-made basement panels are far better than poured-in-place. There is no comparison – the strength the concrete can reach, the reinforcement that is given."

The problem, as Bill sees it, is integrating these changes into the field, and the industry. "It's like any change. Anytime you want to change, you've got to change the mentality to go with it."

Facts speak for themselves. On pre-cast basement walls, service calls, he says, almost disappeared – that wasn't the case years ago with conventionally poured-in-place basements. Pre-made steel interior walls are built to precise dimensions, reducing overall waste – a savings passed on to customers.

The Whiz Kid's garage-bound play and his tinkerings were becoming like other technological innovations rooted in the late 1970s and early 1980s: Largely unseen but vitally important to everyday life.

Improvements in housing technology include steel studs. Besides steel's many benefits, there's less waste, meaning cost-savings for the customer.

As years pass, the homes with Pultrim still look fresh.

Eureka Insight

Bill's pending patent on Pultrim describes a pre-formed, fiberglass-based, low-maintenance, paintable trim that lasts longer and performs better than other trim products. It draws on technology developed in the automotive and aerospace industries.

It is a leap forward, focusing on parts of the house not usually considered, especially when it comes to offsetting the increased costs of a new product. Because Pultrim is prepainted, the homeowner doesn't have to worry about the finish. It will never dull or dent like aluminum. It creates an intrinsic value, allowing Pulte Homes to say: These houses are more valuable, because they are different. They don't need maintenance. As years pass, the whole neighborhood still looks fresh.

Bill knows the risks. He understands the issues. He continues to help create products to improve the company's performance. Pulte culture – embracing change – will be what keeps the company in the forefront of the homebuilding industry.

One of Bill's favorite stories about the auto industry points to the future of housing, and the need for the industry always to look ahead.

"There were once 450 automobile manufacturers in the country," Bill says, "and the Big Three were not known as the Big Three. They automated the assembly process and began making a better quality car. When industrialization improved quality and lowered price, then you had the Big Three. The same thing is going to happen in home building."

But, what housing can't do, he says, is fall asleep and let competitors catch up, like the domestic auto industry has done today.

"We always need to look ahead at new ways and new thinking, not just to keep up, but to stay ahead," Bill says.

This Whiz Kid is a builder trying to solve problems of the new century, taking a cue from other industries while encouraging the use of innovation to soar beyond the competition. He is working to help change mindsets because these changes will require new tools, new applications, and new skills.

As we see oil prices increase and energy concerns grow, as quality and value become ever more important to the consumer, and as on-site labor becomes harder to find, industrialization and improved supply chain dynamics become more essential to the home building industry.

"The characteristic of all these efforts is that he's visionary in his thinking," says a Pulte executive. It would not be the first time Bill, tinkering, has led us where no one else ventured to go.

"We always need to look ahead at new ways and new thinking, not just to keep up, but to stay ahead."

Still The Whiz Kid

Over the years, many vendors have asked Bill for his opinion of products and how to make them better. He appreciates inventions showing simplicity of thought, use, and solution. Bill's office is cluttered with building materials and products including those he's tinkering with in order to better understand how Pulte's building process could be improved.

"Bill, at heart, is truly a craftsman," says a company executive. "And yet, he's constantly innovating. He loves that stuff."

"He has an engineer's mind for detail, product performance, and process, and an artist's flair for design, balance, and flow," says another Pulte executive. "Most people are lucky if they have one of those traits. He has all of them – plus a visionary outlook."

All Bill asks for, when giving ideas to vendors, is that the product be made at a competitive price and save time or material. His main goal is always to build a better home for the customer through either better product performance, richer design detailing, or more competitive pricing.

In the past, he never cared that companies took his ideas to the general market since he was just improving the product from his own experiences.

Meanwhile, his eurekas keep coming.

His Universal Rake Ridge Cap invention, patent pending, came to him while he was building a vacation cottage a few years ago on Michigan's Mullet Lake. On the drive back to the home site after having lunch at a restaurant, Bill was riding in the backseat with his eyes closed. His companions thought he was sleeping.

But, in fact, he was contemplating how to trim a difficult cut at the peak of a gable. Suddenly, Bill opened his eyes and exclaimed, "I've got it!" And then described a round-topped adjustable cap that worked, covering the angles of the cut and making the seams look trimmed.

Over time, Bill has given away many ideas, and in at least one instance after the idea was patented Bill significantly improved the idea. The part was created by a company in Utah that sought Bill's input on the Integral Fascia and Vented Soffit, an aluminum fascia and soffit forming a single piece of material. Bill visited the company and made suggestions from a builder's point of view. Today, manufacturers in the aluminum industry make many products like this.

But after that Utah visit, Bill kept thinking about the product, and in typical Bill Pulte fashion, his Pultrim, by using the pultrusion manufacturing process, solved issues the integral frieze hadn't solved. He included crisper design details, hidden attachment points, and no wood backers – all of which improved the look, the cost, and the quality of the original product, which years before he had worked on in Utah. Bill always seeks to make things better … and never stops turning them over in his mind.

He designed specs for a new window and pushed the window industry to use more Pultruded or similar technology. "He's working on the world's best window," says a Pulte executive. "It never leaks, never needs painting."

When housing industry history is written, Bill Pulte's contribution may have been in providing a perspective on building innovation that could only come from a man who grew up in Detroit: That a home can be built exactly like a car. Its high-quality, precision parts will perform better, last longer, and be cheaper to make on a manufacturing line.

The concepts the Whiz Kid hammered out in his garage in the 1980s could someday be realized.

Bill will always have stuff piled-up in his office, working toward his dream of perfect homes, built in half the time they're built today, with quality impossible for competitors to duplicate.

"Bill created a climate of trying to change things, and it has always been like that," says a Pulte executive. "When history unfolds, the fact that he had the guts to go ahead and try these things, that's what will matter."

Chapter Five
The Teacher

Decades of home building haven't dulled Bill Pulte's enthusiasm for putting a house together. He still does frame walks, which typically take an hour. Bill puts in three. He grabs a tape measure and walks to the end of a wall, or scoops up a hammer and knocks a stud out of a wall – long before he'll ask someone to do it for him.

He points out fine details as he goes. His enthusiasm never dims, no matter how many homes he sees. *"Do you follow me?"* Bill asks. Bill understands the truth in the statement that unchallenged allegiance to ideas blinds us, and only with wonder, with open minds, can we break through to new possibilities. Bill's wonder encompasses everything about the home, from the footings to the eaves. For the business of home building, his wonder never ceases.

With Bill, it's never enough to do something. Everything contains a purpose, a reason, an underlying value. Every story carries a moral. Every home, every person, bears a story, within.

"Let me take you back," Bill usually begins, sharing the big picture, how PVC piping used to be galvanized or cast iron, or how the back deck replaced the front porch. He could be talking to new recruits, division presidents, college professors, career counselors, or educators from across the country.

For the last group, he'll add: "What I've learned through history, I want to use to make better decisions going forward. But I don't have any real interest in going back like some old college superstars. They still revel in their old glories like that's the only thing that matters. They never live in the present.

"By the way, I didn't make it to college."

During his company presentations, at the end, inevitably, a slide illuminates the screen: "One thing to remember: My name is Bill. I'm here to help you."

Says a Pulte executive: "When people realize that he's not just a figurehead, that he really cares genuinely about us doing the right things out in the field – you know – the sticks and bricks … it makes an incredible impression."

Bill has been helping for more than 50 years, and it is as teacher, as ambassador, as embodiment of company culture, that he leaves his legacy.

How will this healthy pride, Bill's values and know-how, become ingrained in all? Through the simplicity of his message. Everyone gets it.

Bill loves numbers, so uses them when he teaches, in the Five Talents, the Five P's, the Seven Rules of Design, and the Eight Sets of Eyes. He is fond of "always" and "never" preambles.

"When you walk into a house, you should *always* be able to look through and see a window," he says. "That makes it feel bigger. You should *always* have a foyer that welcomes you, even in a small home."

"That's Bill's way of keeping things simple," says another executive – *Always* do this. *Never* do that. The idea is, don't make it any more complex than it needs to be."

As participants in Bill's wonder-filled adventure, we know to always follow in his footsteps, never prideful of our achievements, yet confident in making decisions, taking risks, and becoming better at the Pulte Way.

We work, we grow. If we are lucky, we find Bill's cherished inner peace, from which all good decisions flow.

"My name is Bill," he says. "*I'm here to teach – that's my job.*"

Manning Brooms And Bulldozers

Bill has been teaching since his long-grown kids were learning to tie their shoes. Bill remembers when *he* fumbled with his laces.

"If my dad taught us to tie our shoes, you tied your shoes from then on," Bill says. "No matter how much in a hurry we might have been to get somewhere. You did it again and again," Bill says. "All of a sudden, you knew how to tie your shoes. You got confidence."

If there was one quality Bill wanted to instill in his children, it was confidence, and he built that, experience after experience. He wants the same for employees of Pulte Homes.

Do it right the first time is a Pulte maxim that builds confidence. Bill fiercely instilled that self-possession in his 14 kids, whether they were planning day trips, or working to pay for a used car. He wants the same, today, from Pulte's new employees, or from the company's newest managers. It's a trait nestled in his exacting nature.

One of Bill's sons recalls recently hanging a pot rack with his dad, and even though there was room to fudge, Bill laid it out exactly. "So even though we had all this play, he had to lay it out to the eighth of an inch," says Bill's son. "The guy has not changed."

Bill's kids learned to be as exacting in their communication.

"He is very thorough when he communicates with the trades," says one of Bill's sons, also a builder. "I remember, as a kid, I was cleaning up one of the job sites and he came out of his *Mustang* and said, 'Son, you're doing a good job. But you know, you're not cleaning up thoroughly, you're not cleaning up 100%. When sweeping a house, there's a lot of sawdust in the corners, so when I say sweep it out, clean it thoroughly.'

"Now, even with my own workers," says Bill's son, "when I say sweep a house, I can show them how to sweep it thoroughly. And that was the way my Dad always did things."

Another son says his father's philosophy was to understand how to communicate with everyone – from the guy sweeping up, to the guy at the top. "As a little boy, I can remember Dad working right alongside the guys at Pulte Homes, building houses," he says. "If they didn't understand something … he was right beside them. He'd jump out and grab the hammer: 'This is what I am talking about.' Or, I can remember him getting on bulldozers and showing guys: 'This is what I mean.'"

Friends, family, and co-workers all know Bill rarely gets angry. "In fact, while I'm arguing with you," he'll say, "I'm not mad at you. I'm just giving you a different opinion."

Bill always provides concrete examples. "If I were doing this, here's what I'd do," he might explain. If he sees something done, but not well, he'll pose a question, without judgment: "What are you thinking?"

"Everything's a lesson with my Dad," says one of Bill's daughters. "If you can take it and put a spin on it, then it is a learning tool."

"My mother or father never said you had to be home at 9 o'clock or whenever," Bill says. "They just said, 'Be home when you should be.' Freedom, with responsibility."

Bill did the same with his kids. With freedom, and responsibility, they grew.

These days, the chairman speaks to 200-plus Pulte Homes' employees at a time. "No matter whether the person has been in the workplace for some time or is a kid right out of college, they hang on his every word," says a company executive.

Bill's focus puts him in each person's presence, wholly and completely. When he is with you, he is with you, giving you dignity, and respect. "That's what I loved about my dad, and I love about him to this day," says one of his daughters. "He would treat you no differently than if you were the president, or the pope."

"By the way, I didn't make it to college."

*"My name is Bill.
I'm here to teach ...
that's my job."*

"Nothing he teaches is not from his own experience and beliefs and grounded in reality," she says. "One of his highest values is common-sense. It's not a matter of what level of education you have or what your background is. You have to look at what's actually going on, and take it from there."

Bill will always take it from there, and find the simplest, easiest way, always asking: *Do you follow me?* It has meaning whenever, or wherever, or to whomever, it is posed.

Because Bill means it, and he wants to *know*.

The Fifth 'P'

It's likely Bill has heard the proverb, "through wisdom a house is built, and by understanding it is established."

A Pulte home is built from thousands of parts with the participation of thousands of people and their collective wisdom. But only by examining the thinking needed to get to a finished product is a home truly understood.

With common-sense as the foundation of Bill's philosophies and maxims, it's hard to argue his principles and philosophies of home building. Many originated with advice from mentors – land developers, real estate brokers, financiers, interior decorators, and architects – all brought up in the School of Hard Knocks. And it was by Bill's own successes and failures that he tweaked these now-proven rules.

One of Bill's bedrock philosophies is that you need to develop a strategic plan, a preamble to any business effort. It's known as the Five P's: Planning, People, Process, Product, and Profit.

In Planning, you examine your strategic and operational campaigns from every angle and then reexamine each angle. "You can make a lot more money with paper and pencil than you can when you're building in the field," Bill says. It's his way of saying: Think long, and hard, then act.

"Windows are a great thing for perception of space ... as is doing away with walls between rooms."

Always And Never

Bill enjoying a margarita – *always* the non-alcoholic variety.

You'll *never* see Bill in a bathing suit.

Or shorts.

Or drinking tea or coffee. Or sipping a cocktail.

He wouldn't touch a French fry. (A donut, maybe.)

He'll never wear ties. (Well, he has been photographed wearing a few. They *never* stay on long.)

"Ties aren't practical," Bill says. "They strain your neck."

Bill will *always* wear something around his neck if it is to make fun of himself, like a bib, for instance, at a party where people are roasting him.

He'll wear it for the whole party.

Bill isn't afraid to look at things in black and white.

In teaching, "he uses words like 'always' and 'never' a lot," says a Pulte executive. "Because life *is* black and white with Bill.

"So he says 'always do this,' 'never do this.' 'Always' and 'never' stick with people. If you just kind of offer an opinion, that doesn't stick.

"But if you say, 'When you walk into a house, you should *always* be able to look through and see a window and make the house feel bigger than what it is,' it sticks with people.

"It's amazing because always or never rules, they are timeless, the business had not changed from that end.

"Always and never are big words with Bill," says the executive. *"And they always have been."*

People participate in the Process – just like a family. At Pulte Homes no one is self-made – man or woman. "If one man thinks he's gonna do it all, he's crazy," Bill says. "But if he gets the right people to help him and support him, make the plan happen, it will happen."

Hiring the right people and giving them the chance to use their skills is freedom with responsibility. When they ask for advice or input, that shows self-confidence, Bill says. And if they don't know, they shouldn't be afraid to ask. As he learned from Carlo, his first mentor, years ago, there's no such thing as a dumb question.

The Process is how you accomplish your plan, and it needs to be thoroughly thought out. Your process will need systems and experts, and require constant reassessment to improve.

Your Plan must be based on all you know both about the customer and the Product, the fourth P. In Pulte's case, that's "A House on a Lot in a Community." Bill warns against "builder mentality" – the cheaper you make a house, the cheaper you can sell it. "But I will tell you," he says, "sometimes it pays to spend money because you'll have more buyers."

The best way to build is to understand your customer, provide value, and keep it simple. "So many times a builder will put things into a house that don't help sell the house and may even hurt the house," Bill says. "You need to look at each item you put into a house to determine whether it gives value to the customer."

How do you provide value? In the land, in the house, and by knowing costs, so you can use your budget wisely. If you *always* know who the customer is and what he or she wants and can afford, and where he or she wants it, and you *always* strive to give the most for the money, you give value.

"I don't want my people to have 'builder's mentality.' That means taking money out, making it cheaper. No. Sometimes you've got to put stuff in to sell more."

Other factors providing value include the obvious: Square footage in smaller houses is extremely valuable. But in large houses, $50,000 invested in additional square footage isn't as valuable as if the same money were put into upgraded specifications. Subtle elements, like perception of space, which can be drastically altered, for instance, by a well-lit, large and open foyer, can make a tremendous difference. "Windows are a great thing for perception of space as are doing away with walls between rooms," he says. As are ceiling heights.

"If you have the right plan, the right people to perform that plan with the right processes and systems and the right product on top of that, those four P's equal the fifth P," Bill says: Profit.

And, keeping it simple, the fifth P requires no explanation.

Third Dimension Thinking

One of earliest steps in home building that sets up opportunities for education and experience is the Eight Sets of Eyes. These are the disciplines that scrutinize a house, on a lot in a community: Marketing, sales, land development, construction, architecture, engineering, interior design, and business.

When a division buys land in a sub-market that strategic marketing has identified for a specific group of buyers, the architects try to find the right plan for those lots, from the plan archives. If they need a new plan for that community, or need to modify existing plans, the new plan needs to be scrutinized. Before working drawings are made, "we build a prototype," says Bill, "and we look at it from the eight sets of eyes."

The prototype is very temporary, as its purpose is just to get an idea of space. Most of the time, it has no roof. However, if roof features are important to the inside, then a roof is put on.

"We wrap it in visquene, a vapor barrier, to make it feel closed in. After we walk through, we tear it down. It may cost us $4,000 to $5,000 to build and tear down, but everybody gets to see it in the third dimension." Many people can't see in three dimensions, he says, so a plan on paper often is useless.

The eight sets of eyes make up the Pulte expertise.

The marketer knows what goes into the home based on research. "Marketing is so misunderstood," Bill says. "Most builders say, here's my product, how do I write the ads?" Instead, he says, marketers should zero in on who the customer is, what they value, what they expect, what they need. Once they answer those questions, then they can think about promoting it.

The sales people examine the home from their perspective. Does everything look right to sell? Are the four bedrooms and three baths in the right place? What about the missing front closet? Does every house need a closet? "If you're in South Florida, you don't necessarily need that front hall closet for coats," Bill says. "You need a back hall closet because you use that more often."

The land developers come into the picture very early. They know they can only build so much on so much property. Is there room for a garage? Does the sewer line come into the house at the right place? Is the driveway on the high side of the lot?

The construction team looks at the house from the inside out. "I have extra 2x4s here and there's no way the sales person can make any sense of that to the customer," Bill says, giving an example. "We have 42 extra studs in this house. The average buyer wonders why. So how can we build a better quality house, but make it more efficient to build, and how do we make the customer understand that?"

Meanwhile, the architect makes sure everything is in proportion. Are the windows balanced or unbalanced? Does the floor plan flow? Can improvements be made? Is there a better way to do it more economically?

The engineer, like the production team, also looks at the structure. He or she might say, we've got a heavy bearing point, and we don't have enough support – what can we do? To take you back, as Bill likes to do, this was important in the 1970s with waterbeds, which put thousands of pounds of water weight over floor joists.

The interior designer might say it's a beautiful room but it's too open, there's no wall space to fit the bed.

The business person is focused on the bottom line: This is great, but can we make money on it? If it's selling for $100,000 and cost $99,500 to build, it's not worth it, the business expert might say. "He could say, no, unless you cut $15,000 out of this house, we can't build it because there's no money in it," Bill says. "That's happened more than once. It's so expensive the way it's laid out that the costs don't warrant it. Or we do build it and we realize that the costs are too high and we can't get the extra price because there's a square box down the street with exactly the same parts and pieces, but is a lot less money."

Together, the eight sets of eyes make up the Pulte expertise.

"I've seen so many MBAs get into the business and fail because they didn't know anything about building. I've seen trade guys fail because they didn't know anything about finance. What makes Pulte different is we combine trade and finance."

Doesn't Hurt To Repeat: What's It Cost?

Knowing and understanding costs and using them wisely is where many people in home building get into trouble – including MBAs, Bill says.

"Now the tradesman, he never thinks about some of these things," Bill says. "He knows all about direct costs – the costs of the brick, the cost of the concrete. But he forgets about the taxes he's paying on the property, the interest he's paying on the borrowed money. He forgets all the indirect costs that he can't see and touch."

And then, at the year's end, that same guy wonders why he didn't make a dime. "Well, he didn't include all these costs," says Bill.

And then there are hidden costs.

"Those are costs that just don't normally show up," Bill says. "In northern climates we have to heat the house in wintertime. I can have a house where a tradesman left the windows open all night long. So I'm heating the outdoors. I don't get a nickel for that. But that's a hidden cost.

"You had no idea the cost was going to be there, but you have to expect that's going to happen some of the time. So you gotta put contingencies in for that kind of costing.

"Because if you don't, you won't be successful."

Does It Live Well?

Bill's Seven Rules of Design follow similar common-sense, which came from a real estate broker who financed some of Bill's early projects.

"The most important thing is the location of your house," Bill says of the first rule. "Is it in the submarket the buyer wants to buy in?"

Once that's established, does the house have "curb appeal"? So when the customer drives up, he or she says … "Wow! I'm going in."

That "Wow" must extend to the foyer, which should be lofty, well lit, warm, and welcoming.

"Bill has a whole sense of arrival," says a Pulte executive. "He has a keen sense of what an emotional experience home buying is for people."

From their earliest steps into a Pulte home, buyers should see a family room and kitchen in proportion to the house. And the kitchen should be bright, cheerful, and workable. "So many builders think if they use small windows, they can make it cheaper, but all of a sudden, the room becomes dark," Bill says. "A small, dark kitchen is not cheerful." Workable means generous work places between the refrigerator and the sink, the two most used appliances.

The fifth rule of design covers the master bedroom suite, which has to be in scale to the size of the house, with the master bath right off the suite – for a very common-sense reason: "You must put the bath next to the master bedroom and have it connected because mom and dad don't want to get up in the middle of the night and put their robes on," Bill says. "The kids can go down the hall, but not mom and dad."

Living space must be in proportion to the number of people in the house. Kid's bedrooms don't sell houses, Bill says, so they shouldn't be the focal point. "Of course, you've got to make sure the furniture lays out in the kid's bedroom and that there's sufficient closet space," Bill observes. "But, if you've got the right location and curb appeal, mom and dad will get those kids into those bedrooms."

The final question is asked by everyone: *Does the house live well?* The ultimate praise is a simple "yes."

Because then, the house, through wisdom and understanding, sells, as a home.

Personal Touch

When Bill speaks to new hires he knows they need to be inspired and educated in The Pulte Way. He stresses their vital role in the company's future. His detailed colored process charts show them the Big Picture. From the start, Bill wants them to understand the roles of all disciplines, and what people in each discipline do, and how they interact.

His clear thinking has boiled the process down to about 15 pages. The charts give context, explain functions, and establish constant understanding and communication in the company. "It's world class," says a Pulte board member. "It's very well thought out."

Bill's presentations frequently bring standing ovations, and it's not uncommon for new hires to remove nametags for him to sign. Bill could do without the adoration, but thrives on the energy.

"To see the outpouring of emotion is overwhelming," says a Pulte executive. "If you ask later – What did you get out of Bill's talk? What was the highlight? The new employee will say: 'That Mr. Pulte – I'm sorry – I mean Bill, was there. I could tell he wanted to be with us and share all he knows. I wrote to my parents that night. I told them I got to meet the founder, and I've only been with the company a month!'"

"That's the human side of our organization," says the executive. "That is the personal touch that Bill brings to things."

"Marketers should zero in on who the customer is, what they value ... and what they need."

"To teach the business, that's something," says another executive. "But you have to attract the right people first, who want to be part of something, to be part of Pulte's culture. They've seen it. But wow, then when they see it embodied *in the man*, that makes it more real for them."

Bill *is* the man. But a kid all the same, who loves the business as much as he did when he was just getting started, right out of high school.

Humanity Lesson

Bill's lessons in humanity come anytime, anywhere. He sees every interaction as an opportunity, and he treats everyone individually.

"Sometimes Bill underestimates the power behind his actions," says a Pulte executive. "We have recruits from a very junior level to executive level who visit the home office. Bill doesn't know who's a recruit. He'll just be in a hallway and walk by and he'll be the first to stick out his hand.

"Hey, I'm Bill Pulte. How you doin'?"

"It's so powerful," says the executive. "He personally has helped recruit hundreds of people just by that. And he'll talk for 10 minutes.

"He'll get *that* engaged. When you have the chairman and founder of the company doing that, that's powerful."

And yet, Bill will say, "I didn't do anything. It's no big deal."

Maybe not to Bill. But *everything* to the man or woman coming into an organization whose founder is an icon, a legend ... a teacher extraordinaire.

The Average Joe Test

Bill flies a good bit, and one day reading a magazine as he waited for his plane to depart, he took the quiz: "Are You An Average Joe?"

"How many times have you traveled overseas?" the quiz wanted to know. Honest Bill had to circle "five or more." Instantly, he knew: *Not good.*

Survey said: Bill's no Average Joe.

Why is it important for Bill to be "average?"

"I think it speaks to his own humility and the person he is," says a Pulte employee. "It's very important to him. If you're not an Average Joe, you can't relate to people in this business."

Bill takes human relations to heart. Anything that impairs his ability to relate from white-collar executives to hands-on, problem-solving people, on a deep-down "folks" level, hits a man hard who has long ridden in coach, just to chat awhile with Average Joes, to maybe hear what they have to say about homes.

"It bothered him for a minute, but he shook it off," says the employee. "Bill gets over everything. Behaviors are more important than any test in a magazine."

But the word's out: Bill's not average.

We knew that.

Bill connects during a company softball game.
His batting average is, well, average,
and a closely guarded company secret.

"I think the home building business is the greatest business in the United States to be in for a young person today. We've got people at Pulte who five years ago came out of college and are running some of our subdivisions, and in a couple of years are gonna run divisions."

"Real success is going to bed at night knowing you did your very best that day."

Remembering Bill

It has been said that those we most admire have the most influence on us: Someone whose words and actions shed a new light upon our lives, and changed its direction: someone who gave it balance and a meaning that had previously escaped us.

Our contact with this person may have even been brief. Perhaps our observations have been from afar. Yet, who they were, what they stood for, inspired us to want to make the most of our lives.

That's how Bill Pulte would like his legacy left. While his name is barely seen in the expanse of time, his balance and inflection will be felt in our everyday lives.

It will be long-lasting, because in rules and maxims, in stories, true influence always is felt, and through that influence we will discover more of ourselves, and our purpose. And be happy with what we've accomplished.

"Real success is not measured in fame or wealth," Bill says. "It's that you can go to bed at night and say you did the best you could for that day."

Inner peace, the Pulte Way.

Chapter Six
The Leader

Y ou can see it in Bill's baby pictures: Complete confidence. His eyes seem to suggest: You want *me* to stand still?

On his lips: A perfect tough-boy scowl. His right fist: Tight and ready, behind his hip. His left hand: Unclenched, hanging at his side, as if about to point. His feet: Small, but solidly planted.

You can see it in his teenage pictures: Self-assurance, mixed with bright-eyed optimism and joy. *Nothing would beat this kid down. Nothing would stop his momentum. Nothing.*

He has led Pulte Homes with compassion, loyalty, integrity, and fierce determination – the same look of resolve that can be seen in his face when he was just two years old, standing amid dry weeds on good earth.

He started his business in a cyclical industry in Detroit, a city that gave meaning to the words "up-and-down," and "down-and-out." Real estate in an automobile town – you've got to be an optimist to consider it, no?

When he became a production builder, Bill mortgaged all he owned, effectively betting personal wealth and family security on his belief in himself, and what he, and his team, built with their hands.

"He just knew it would work," says a Pulte executive.

How did he know? What makes Bill Pulte a leader confident enough to take such risks? Was it born in him? Was it made?

We may never know the answers, but clues come in the spirit Bill believes leaders at Pulte Homes need to possess. A new leader at Pulte could draft a wish list of Bill's leadership traits; those nurtured in Bill; and over time, the traits Bill has nurtured in others.

Bill at two-years-old:
"You want *me* to stand still?"

Bill has vision. He works hard, but work is fun. He relies on common-sense. He's confident in a crisis. He likes a challenge. He embraces risk. His optimism is boundless.

Bill trusts people. As his kids learned, he assesses talent and shortcomings well. He asks for input. He understands problems. He's mentally tough. He forgoes ego. He's approachable. He motivates people. He makes quick decisions.

He isn't afraid to lead.

Bill has always been a hands-on leader – leaping aboard a bulldozer when he needed to, or scaling a climbing wall, or participating enthusiastically at a holiday party and other company outings. He's the engager. He's the enabler. Be yourself.

Live. Learn. *Have fun.*

Bill is hands off when he needs to be. He no longer desires to run the company from day to day. He'll focus on the big picture. "We've got to play in these new sandboxes," he says. "What are they?"

This is the same man demoted in the U.S. Army for never sewing on his Private First-Class stripe. This is the man who admits he didn't read much – until he was 33. This is a man who accidentally stumbles on a stage, collects himself, and, completely unembarrassed, jokes about the gaffe.

Even when the laugh's on him, as when his muddy tracks were videotaped after he walked through a freshly vacuumed model home, or in a photo showing him awkwardly sitting astride a camel, Bill demonstrates what it means to be a selfless leader.

Bill maintains his presence of mind, no matter the situation, like when his pants split in New York City and he stapled them together, calmly continuing through his first day as the leader of a public corporation. How many chairmen could take a rip like that in stride, and carry on?

Bill would say he's the leader he is because of the leaders with whom he chose to surround himself. He always sought the best people for the job.

But there's no doubt that his humility, his confidence, his clear-eyed optimism, play critical roles in his leadership formula. "Bill never gets down," says a Pulte executive. "He's optimistic and realistic ...

"And he never hesitates to act."

"Be a leader people have the habit of underestimating."

There's *Always* Tomorrow

Bill Pulte is a student of history – recall the Orange Sweater Legend in high school. He loves the History and Biography channels and, it is apparent from what he models, he has studied the traits of history's greatest leaders.

Bill uses certain principles consistently to govern how he leads. He advocates and reaffirms a vision. He circulates among his followers. He builds alliances. He searches out intelligent assistants. He encourages innovation. He persuades rather than coerces. He influences people through stories. He's results driven.

Bill trusts his people. And he seeks to give them room to grow, to make mistakes. "A CEO at a major company had the best answer," he says. "A guy in one of his divisions lost $25 million. Wall Street says, 'When are you going to fire him?' He said, 'Fire him? I just spent $25 million educating him!'"

Bill runs a company that spends hundreds of thousands of dollars each year educating leaders, hopefully, not to make in-the-field mistakes of the $25 million caliber. But Bill knows that for people to grow, they need to get out, make decisions, and be accountable.

When mistakes are made, own up to them, Bill says. "When somebody makes a mistake don't spend a fortune trying to find out who's to blame," he says. "Focus on how to solve the problem and go forward."

Bill's hands-off approach and constant drive to clearly understand the problem make him a perfect mentor, a perfect teacher, a leadership ambassador.

"I've been around a lot of senior and chief executives," says a Pulte vice president. "I have never seen the type of leadership, the type of hands-off approach that he has. The hands are off, but he's there when you need him.

"He knows to surround himself with good people; he knows he has to give those people room to grow and make mistakes … and be responsible and accountable. Lastly, he has this fathering, nurturing peace in his soul that is calming. It prevents him from acting like any other chairman. He turns anger into a positive.

"Bill's brilliance comes out in a crisis," the executive adds. "It comes from his comfort level with who he is, and that he knows he will always try to do the right thing by people. He knows that if everyone's intentions are positive, good prevails.

"Bill's brilliance comes out in a crisis," the executive adds. "It comes from his comfort level with who he is, and that he knows he will always try to do the right thing by people. He knows that if everyone's intentions are positive, good prevails.

"When people are frustrated or frantic, he's the guy who knows it can't be that bad. *He's been there. He's done that.* What we considered crises, he considered bumps in the road."

Bill's optimism pervades any difficult situation. The expansiveness of his thinking, his always-and-never principle, kicks in. He *always* looks to the far side of the problem. *Never* forget. There's *always* tomorrow.

Don't Check The Wind

Part of Bill's hands-off approach and trust comes from his need for his leaders to be candid with their thoughts and feelings. "Good people aren't 'yes men' or 'yes women,'" he says. They don't hesitate to tell him when he's wrong. They give honest counsel. They're leaders.

Although Bill's confidence was formed at an early age, it grew over the years through his success in surmounting obstacles and solving problems.

He looks for people who have developed a similar sturdy backbone. "Bill wants people who aren't afraid to tell it like it is," says a Pulte board member. "That means people have to be very self-confident."

The leaders at Pulte Homes look for others who share their value system and will embrace the leadership principles Bill has taught them: Treat people right, have some humility and be willing to share the credit.

Bill knows that the humble have a gift: They are able to find something worth admiring in the commonplace or apparently uninteresting. They can see the wonder in simple things and qualities others fail to notice. The humble are given more to listening than to speaking.

"Be a leader people have the habit of underestimating," Bill says.

He likes to be challenged and has a genuine desire to get others' opinions about why something should be done a different way. "To me, the most unhelpful kind of employee to have is one who agrees with you all the time. Do you want somebody who will say, 'That's a good idea.' Or, 'I think that won't work and here's why.'"

"You can't be one of these guys who spend 80 percent of the time getting that last 20 percent of the information. By that time, the decision is made."

Speaking Up, Not Shutting Up

How do you encourage executives to create an environment where people aren't afraid to challenge you?

Bill has the answer.

"You have to continually tell people that they can challenge you," he says. "As a leader, you have to admit when you're wrong and say. 'That's a better idea than I had, and I appreciate it,' or, 'I was dead wrong. And this idea is better.'"

That honesty only produces good results.

"If people know that you've admitted something was better or you were wrong and you apologize, that gets around," Bill says.

"But until that atmosphere becomes a normal thing, you have to repeat it. And if they know you changed your mind, or if someone shares that you admitted you were wrong and apologized, that gets around fast."

A good example of this is his 'focus groups.' Bill is always looking to simplify the options for customers – whether toilets, bathtubs, or any number of things. "He'll say, 'which of these two designs do you like better, and why?'" says an employee. "But, he does not want people to say, 'I like this one' because they get a hint that might be what he likes. Most times, he and I don't agree."

Bill listens, and always ends conversations, no matter the discussion, with "thank you," because he is, indeed, thankful for the talents each person brings to his thorny problem of the day.

"The best kind of an employee is the one who will give the correct answer, whether the boss wants to hear it or not," he says. "If you give the boss a different view and the back-up, you're a very valuable employee," he says.

But a leader must create an environment where his people feel free to voice their opinions and problems. And once a problem is resolved, a good leader leaves it behind and moves on.

"Bill's not going to sit at the dinner table and talk about the issues that happened today at work that he's still fretting about," says a Pulte executive. "He feels he's done. He feels he's always going to do the right thing based on the information he has."

Trust And Change

Bill has never shirked away from being straightforward, some would say blunt, with his leaders. "Bill is doing it to teach, not to be punitive," says a Pulte executive. "It's a great experience for any leader because Bill wants people to challenge him. If he's wrong, tell him he's wrong. He'll respect you for that."

Bill remembers the years when three key executives led the company. "There was barely a conflict," he says, "but we should have had more quarrels than we did. I've learned that one man's decisions aren't always the best. Even if he ends up getting his way, the issue always should be aired a little bit."

Bill complimented one leader this way: "His integrity was there. He had the facts when he did argue with you and he would shut up if the facts were against him."

"Bill wants leaders like himself,"an executive says. "Someone able to handle criticism and laugh at himself. He doesn't get caught up in taking criticism personally. If he can see that what's being said makes sense, will lead to greater efficiencies, or less mistakes, or, more importantly, a better quality home, that's what truly matters."

But, change is the crucible in which Bill inspires his leaders to achieve higher goals. "All the major reorganizations, he came to us saying, 'we're going to change,'" says a Pulte executive. "We need to reorganize. The business is booming now, but now's the time to change."

"That's confidence. He felt that his leaders could make the change successfully and carry out the duties and responsibilities to drive successful change. *That's the power behind Bill Pulte.*

"He always sensed we would get caught up in our own success, and he challenged us to the next level," says the executive. "If we saw we could grow 10 percent, he'd say why not 25? We'd say, we don't have the land. He'd say, why not get the land? He always challenged us."

His trust is substantial.

One employee says Bill never thinks twice about giving her the key to his house or asking her to deposit his company bonus checks at the bank. "I think Bill looks at everybody and knows good is in everybody," she says. "He doesn't see bad in anybody."

"I've learned that one man's decisions aren't always the best.... The issue always should be aired a little bit."

Bill wants leaders to stay approachable, no matter their title.

"He knows that because of his position people won't always freely open up, but he sincerely wants them to," says an executive. "He talks a lot about getting clarity, and that means forgetting yourself and focusing on the problem."

There may never be a Bill Pulte Leadership Center, but there ought to be. The first rule: *Check your ego at the door.*

Passion For Day-to-Day

Having vision, being a boss who takes part, having fun, using street smarts, and hiring smarter people who are "doers" and problem solvers, all make up the Pulte approach to leadership.

"A good leader doesn't just delegate and walk away," Bill says. "The leaders at Pulte are willing to get their hands dirty." And Pulte hires leaders who don't view work as work. Bill wants them to share his perspective: "I'd give up golf any day to work. I always have fun. I've always enjoyed what I'm doing."

Bill wants his people to share his passion for what they do day-after-day-after-day.

While a good leader has vision, he understands he needs to motivate people to execute the vision. "People make the whole thing work," Bill says. "Nothing else."

Much of that execution depends on street smarts, Bill says: "A guy or gal who's got street smarts and common-sense will get the job done. I would rather have somebody who is intelligent and with lots of common-sense and street smarts than someone who is only book smart."

Bill believes there's always someone who could do something better than him, but he's never met a person who had no weaknesses. So, when Bill talks about hiring smarter people, they're smarter in certain areas, and they form a team. The team is a concentration of strengths, and weaknesses. He wants to mitigate the weaknesses, and leverage the strengths.

"I don't like to carry grudges. In fact, while I'm arguing with you, I'm not mad at you. I'm just giving you a different opinion."

"We want ideas because that's why we brought you in," he says. "We brought you in because you're smarter or are eventually going to be smarter than a lot of people around you in certain areas, but not every area. That's a mistake, by the way, a lot of people make.

"Say you're a sales person but your skill to select people has never been fine-tuned. All of a sudden, you become a sales manager. Now you think you are supposed to be an expert at selecting people to be sales persons. Dead wrong. You have no more talent for selecting people the day after you became sales manager than the day before when you were a sales person.

"So many times people think their position gives them a talent that they don't have – their egos say: 'I'm the sales manager now. I'm supposed to do this.' No. You're not supposed to do it if you don't have the talent. Get somebody to help you."

Asking for input and advice doesn't show weakness, it shows confidence, Bill says. "That means you're strong."

Leaders Are "Doers"

Bill was never afraid to hire or consult people better than himself, even from his first day as an entrepreneur when he turned to Carlo, his builder-mentor.

"I designed most of Pulte's plans for years," Bill says. "But there was one expert, Bob Wood, if I ever had a problem, I'd get him on the phone and we'd discuss it, because I trusted his input. If you were a customer of his and you wanted to force a window here or do something that would kill the design, he'd say, 'Bill, go find another architect, because it's wrong.'"

So how did Bill keep intact the egos of people who need confidence, yet humility, to serve?

Bill – always climbing to new heights.

> *"Smart people do smart work if they have a smart boss."*

"Sometimes I didn't," he admits. "An ego can be hidden. But, if they didn't like openness and feedback, they usually didn't last long. If people value openness, they want advice. They realize they don't know everything. So they're just as willing to learn as other people on the team."

One strength Pulte leaders must have is problem solving – they must identify and resolve problems quickly.

"One of the best employees I ever had could not solve a problem but was great at identifying problems. He was in sales and he could sell, he could close. What a great talent he had, and he knew when he had a problem. And 50 percent of solving any problem is knowing you've got it" Bill says.

"So it's important that you have people around you who understand when you've got problems. And even if they can't solve them, they may be more valuable than those who can but don't realize they've got them."

Hire people smarter than yourself, Bill says. Don't worry about who gets credit. Don't play politics. Smart people do smart work if they have a smart boss.

"We want doers," he says. "We don't want people who get bogged down in debate. We want people who get it done. We want to get as much information from everybody as we can, but somebody has to make the decision."

Bill says he once had an executive who wasn't a strategic thinker. But if given a plan and direction, "Let me tell you, he would get the job done no matter what it took. On the other hand, I had another guy smart as heck at strategic thinking and planning, but he never got anything done."

Know Your Limits

"One of the biggest mistakes I made as a manager, is I stayed with people too long," Bill Pulte says. "I just wanted to give them another chance.

"A lot of those people were the right person at the time. But they didn't grow to the same extent we did.

"If we had stayed at the same size or shape as when they came aboard, they would still be excellent employees. But it's hard for most people to admit that they've reached the limits of their abilities and stay there. They always want to go the next notch up.

"Maybe it's because it means more money or more prestige or something. But they would be far happier if they just stayed right there and consistently got satisfaction from accomplishing what they could."

Take Flack, Radiate Trust

"An awful lot of big egos and an awful lot of yelling and screaming really hide the insecurity of the leader," the chairman says. "That person usually has a poor self-image and pulls all these fancy tricks. Someone who has a lot of self-confidence and security doesn't have to yell and scream."

It sounds simple, but Bill also knows a leader needs to take charge.

He tells his leaders: "You're in a leadership position, you've built credibility, be straightforward with your people – this is what you have to do."

"It just never occurred to me," says one executive whom Bill "schooled" on that point one day, "to straightforwardly tell someone exactly what you want them to do. It sounds so obvious. You say, well, how can you lead an organization and not tell people what to do?

"Oftentimes you forget your experience trumps the other person's experience. Just like sometimes I love to be told what I need to do – you forget you need to tell others. Particularly when tough decisions need to be made.

"Bill gives people the courage," the executive says, "to make those tough decisions by just saying: You can do that. Go ahead, make the decision."

Now, the leader who never got far in the Army, who never got far in college, who never wanted fame or fortune, only enough to support his family, has soared to heights that even he never imagined.

"A good leader has to radiate trust. He has to demonstrate over and over again that he's for his people."

He earns standing ovations from his employees, industry leaders seek his advice, college professors and students hang on his words. But, to Bill, none of that matters.

To him, being a leader isn't about success, it's about results and helping people enjoy their work as they rise to a level of competence that gives everyone satisfaction. It's about people and building the confidence that comes from leading, or being led, well.

"A leader has to be respected by his people, and they need to know that he's with them all the way," Bill says. "He's not sitting back and letting them take all the flack.

"A good leader has to radiate trust," he says. "He has to demonstrate over and over again that he's *for his people.*"

The Bill Pulte Story

The Quiet Giver, at the door of a modest Guatemalan home. Bill has always appreciated the chance to bring children happiness.

Chapter Seven
The Quiet Giver

B ill Pulte, the man who for half a century had made his fortune building Americans their homes, stood in the heart of a 200-acre garbage dump in Guatemala City, Guatemala.

It was the middle of summer. The stench – unbearable. The flies – black and buzzing. And yet, Bill saw children and infants foraging through the trash and competing with rats for half-eaten food. Entire families rummaged for discarded junk they could sell for their survival.

Bill's thought was singular and purposeful: "Let's get the kids out of here first."

It wasn't long before Bill's generosity and effort, through Central American Ministries, pulled 4,000 people – mainly children – out of the dump. They're now cared for in nurseries and schools, and many live in modest homes.

"Philanthropy" in Greek means "love of humanity." For Bill Pulte, love of his fellow man is a consequence of who he is and a natural derivative of his personal success. He has been called by one of many beneficiaries, *"a pearl of great price."*

Bill is the most unadorned of philanthropists. You'll find no Bill Pulte plaques on any building. Yet, near and far, his quiet, private gifts have provided shelter, sustenance, and restored dignity to men, women, and children.

Bill craves anonymity rather than public appreciation of what he's made possible, how he has intimately and personally changed the world.

"The font of his charity, or part of it, is that Bill loves people," says Karen Pulte.

"His motivation flows from humble gratitude to God and a firm conviction that since he has been greatly blessed, he, in turn, must share with others," says Adam Cardinal Maida, Roman Catholic Archbishop of Detroit. "I am always amazed at all the good he does in hidden ways, behind the scenes, never drawing attention to himself."

How Bill became a champion of the poor and destitute stems from his own Depression-era childhood. Over time, the fire of his charity only grew.

"Let's get the kids out of here first."

The Bill Pulte Story   123

*"Whatever you do,
do it with integrity
and honesty."*

Road To The Good Life

Why does Bill Pulte give, and how does he give?

One of his daughters insists that her dad feels everyone has a responsibility to each other, and to the world.

"He thinks we should not be so worried about what we get out of something," she says. "Be more worried about what you can *give*. Because in giving, it will come back to you tenfold. It's not the reason we do it, but you feel better when you give that way.

"I think there's a common thread from my dad. My dad is not a perfect man. He is a human being and made mistakes. Not a lot, but he made them. But there are some common threads from the time I was small: Be fair. Be a person of integrity. Don't lie. Give to others."

Bill Pulte, she says, wants young people to know that they should do what they have a passion for, and goodness will follow. "Don't worry about getting your name in spotlights," she says. "Don't worry about making all the money. Don't worry about making the home runs. That will all come – if you do what you love."

"But pick what you're good at. Whatever you do, do it with integrity and honesty. That's how he has lived his life."

The Contemplative Fixer

Just as in his business, in philanthropy, Bill "wants to get on with fixing things," says Fr. Don Vettese, S.J., founder of Central American Ministries.

After all, as his children learned so early, *there's no such thing as can't*.

It was Fr. Vettese who took Bill to the Guatemala City dump. "He is impatient to make progress," says the priest, who is also president of St. John's Jesuit School in Toledo, Ohio. "This is not to say he denies problems. He just wants to *act* as he's *thinking*."

Philanthropy to Bill is private because it stems from his heart. "He gives cheerfully," says Fr. Vettese. "The left hand doesn't know what the right hand is doing."

Pulte Homes has charitable giving programs, but Bill Pulte's service goes beyond those efforts. The Pulte Family Charitable Foundation helps the poor, the homeless, the elderly, and neglected and abused children. The foundation seeks to eliminate poverty and bestow dignity; provide tools for work; help the imprisoned, including victims of domestic violence and racism; provide food and shelter for the poor; and provide companionship and counseling to the dying, and their families.

"He believes everything he has is a gift," says one of Bill's daughters. "He doesn't know why God gave him this responsibility, and he truly looks at this as a responsibility. He is a steward of what God has given him."

Fr. Vettese suggests that while Bill doesn't want, and prefers not to have recognition, he has told the chairman: "We need it! Other people need to see what you do. Maybe that's the last thing you can give: A wonderfully positive example, at your own expense. That's a sacrifice, maybe a final sacrifice."

I'm No Saint

Bill Pulte is the first to admit he wears no halo. He'll tell you he's far from flawless, and he'll add that his children might have a few stories to humble him. Raising 14 kids while running and growing a business from dozens to hundreds to thousands of employees meant that even the most saintly of men would be tested, and make wrong decisions. And Bill's passion for his work may have tended to divert his attentions.

"I think he looked at us as his responsibilities, as in 'I've got to provide for my family,'" says one son. "Put food on the table, a roof over our heads, stuff like that ... With so many kids, our father had to throw you out there. 'I'll teach you once,' and that's it."

"But he's a human being," says another child. "As he's grown, he has taught us to have mercy and that he is not a perfect human being. I always thought he was perfect and wondered why he didn't run for President of the United States."

Like many fathers of his generation, Bill's not a big telephone or e-mail user, but he lets his kids know they can *always* call. "I am sure he's thinking about us every day and prays for us every day," says one son.

Bill does indulge himself: A second home in Florida to get away from the Michigan winters, a new car every few years (usually the most unusual color combination no one will buy, usually with a mock convertible top, always with wire wheels added later), and a new golf club now and again. As most employees know, clothes aren't an indulgence – he has been known to re-sole his shoes four or five times, and even buy his colorful sweaters on eBay.

He loved his ice cream and strawberry milkshakes until health concerns relegated those treats to "special occasions." Although Karen Pulte notes Bill's list of special occasions seems to keep growing.

"We all make mistakes. You've got to learn from that and move on."

Sacrifice, And Christmas Joy

One of Bill Pulte's sons suspects the birth of his father's philanthropy occurred in his earliest years as a builder.

Bill's first philanthropic act was to build a home for his parents. It would be his second house and the first home his parents had ever owned. "I showed them how they could afford to build a house," he says, "and built it for them … they were delighted."

It would be a special gift within that home, however, that would affect him the rest of his life.

It was late Christmas Eve, probably 1951.

The 19-year-old Bill was quietly installing a dishwasher. It was a surprise for his mother, Marguerite, the person in his life he most respected, a woman who gave of her life – to her children, to her husband, to her family, to her community, to her church. And who, with six kids, washed a lot of dishes.

Bill's early foray into homebuilding had given him the means to make this gift, but giving it helped him understand that charity was something he needed to nurture the rest of his life.

When his mother woke up Christmas morning and saw the dishwasher, she started to cry. They were tears of joy. Bill, immediately, felt his own joy. He would later be heard to say many times: "That was the first time I understood there was more joy in giving than receiving."

"I understood there was more joy in giving than receiving."

Bill with his mother, father and brother Tim, two days after being drafted into the army.

Sharing Christmas with the Pultes.

Instilling The Sense Of Sharing

When Bill's own family ballooned from nine to 14 children after his marriage to the late Joan McDonald, he saw that one of his most important responsibilities was sharing with his kids his greatest gift – his faith. The lessons encased within that kernel of love: Being leaders; being bold and having the courage to take a stand on what's right; and being charitable.

Bill stood as a pillar of right and wrong, teaching mercy and compassion for people with less. In his wisdom, he knew that by teaching his children to give, they would give of their whole spirit, and that spirit would grow as they became adults.

To this day, his children say it was only through their father's gentle – and sometimes less-than-gentle – parenting that they've kept that gift of faith.

The charity portion of faith wasn't so easy to grasp at first. Especially for the youngest children when it came to giving up Christmas gifts so other families, who couldn't afford gifts, could receive them.

"We were very blessed with the things we had," says one of Bill's sons. "We never had to want for food or clothing. Like most kids, we really didn't know how good we had it."

"When Dad and Joan got married, they wanted to teach us how to be philanthropic," says a Pulte daughter. "When it started, we all moaned and groaned. But it became the highlight of Christmas."

Bill and his wife collected all the money that would have been spent on the 14 children, and took on a family Christmas project. This went on for about 15 years. One year they visited a home for the mentally challenged, and another year, they visited a Vietnamese immigrant family, who, they learned through their church, was in need.

Another year – because being a good steward meant not just giving money, but spending time and talent with those in need – they visited a nursing home and gave presents to people who didn't have any living relatives. "We sang Christmas carols with them," says one of Bill's daughters.

"We were living Christmas," says another child of Bill's. "We were being taught: It's not what you have, it's what you can give. It showed us that the world was greater than ourselves, even though we were just little kids."

Painted Rocks & Handmade Hats

Meanwhile, at home, everyone got one gift from Santa – and everyone received the same thing. The Pultes remember that first year: The gift was a rolled-up plastic sled for each of them. Later, there were lots of sweaters.

"But also what we did, in lieu of everybody getting store-bought presents, is we made gifts," says a Pulte daughter. "We picked a name out of a hat and you made that person a present."

The Pulte kids got creative. They made scarves, hats, scrapbooks, and needlepoint designs. Dad crafted jewelry boxes, and wooden and wire crosses. Joan stitched afghan blankets.

Karen Pulte recalls that 20 years later, Bill re-made a crucifix for one of his daughters with soldering wire, because hers was destroyed. He gave it to her for Christmas and she cried. Once again, the joy it brought Bill was priceless.

Of course with the gift grab-bag method, you never knew what you'd get. "If your name was picked by one of the little kids, they made you a painted rock," recalls one child. "I have a beautiful piece of artwork from one of my stepbrothers."

Often, it would take the Pultes as long as six hours to carefully open the gifts, and thank the givers.

Bill, the proud grandfather.

Good Instincts

The words rattled in Fr. Don Vettese's head.

An 18-year-old kid in his Boys Hope home in Detroit had killed someone.

Fr. Vettese called Bill Pulte. Bill was a benefactor the priest could always count on.

"Well, that's why you're doing it – because these kids are in trouble," Bill told him. "And this boy made a mistake. And we all make mistakes. You've got to learn from that and move on. I'm happy you're working with people who are in trouble."

Then, the boy was released from jail, having served his time. "He needed a lot, and had spent 10 years, from age 18 to 28, in jail," the priest says.

"I called Bill again. I said, 'You remember him?' He's going to have to get a job. I have to do something."

"Well, listen," Bill says. "Don't get him a fast-food job in a ghetto. Make him go to school, because if he goes and gets a low-end job, he's going to be tempted into crime again. And if he goes to school, he'll have hope for a long-term future. He'll be less likely to get into trouble."

"I'll tell you something," Fr. Vettese says. "That kid today is on the college dean's list, in his second year with a 3.5 G.P.A. I never would have worked to get him into school and funded if Bill had not told me to do that. He cared about the kid. He had good instincts about how to help.

"Quite frankly, I discovered over the years, and I've known him for close to 30 years now, good things happen if you follow his directions. He has never given me bad advice."

To this day, the young man has no idea of Bill Pulte's influence in his life.

"Quite frankly, I discovered over the years, and I've known him for close to 30 years now, good things happen if you follow his directions. He has never given me bad advice."

– Fr. Don Vettese, S.J.

A Legacy Of Joy

As the kids learned about their own philanthropy, they slowly learned about their Dad's: One red sweater he wears is a gift from the nuns who schooled his children. Their simple kindness was a thank you for a convent he built them in 1965.

Bill helped Fr. Vettese start Boys Hope, now Boys Hope Girls Hope, an intervention home for at-risk, yet academically capable kids. Its mission is to help these young people realize their potential by providing family-like homes and quality education. Boys Hope Girls Hope now serves communities in 16 cities in the U.S. and in Brazil, Guatemala, and Ireland. Program alumni have graduated from the finest colleges, some becoming doctors, ministers, police officers, and teachers.

For years, the poorest churches in the Detroit archdiocese as well as starving families in the inner city, have all benefited from Bill Pulte's quiet compassion.

As a classroom mentor to inner-city school children, Bill spends several days with students over the school year. On a recent visit, Karen Pulte heard kids whispering in the hallways: "Hey guys, hey guys, that's Mr. Pulte!' They stop, and Bill goes to shake their hands, and you see these boys looking him straight in the eye, as he's taught them, and he says, 'Attaboy, attaboy!' And these kids are glowing."

Some insight into the impact of Bill Pulte's charity comes from Fr. Vettese. "He always wants to know what it will take to make things better, and then he does it," the priest says. "Bill never complains and never wastes time feeling sorry for the people or himself."

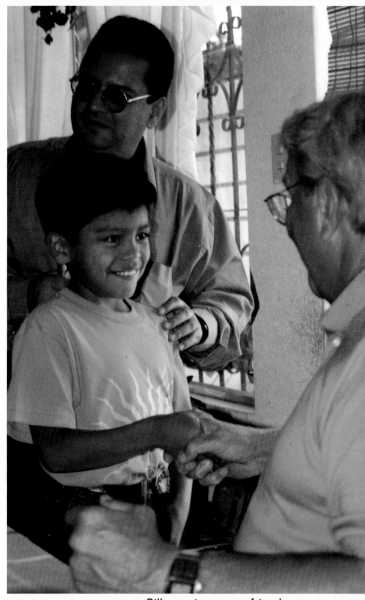

Bill greeting a new friend at
Boys Hope Girls Hope in Guatemala City.
"Hi, my name is Bill — what's yours?"

Heart Of Gold ... Feet Of Muck

Bill Pulte's charity extends to the simplest matters.

One Pulte employee recalls the time a secretary was flying to Houston from Detroit for the weekend.

Bill was on the same flight, and was upgraded to first class (Bill would never pay for first class). Before getting on the plane, he insisted that the woman sit in his first-class seat, and that he take her coach seat. "I'll have more opportunity to do it than you," he told her.

Despite her resistance, Bill persisted. She ended up in first class, with the chairman of the board in coach. "That's just Bill," says the employee who relates the story.

Bill clearly doesn't hesitate to help anyone in need, especially when it's a matter that goes straight to his tradesman heart.

A Pulte executive recalled a phone call from his wife, one night when he was out of town. She exclaimed: "Bill just showed up at the front door! He's now in the yard in three feet of snow, on his hands and knees trying to figure out where the odor is coming from."

The executive had purchased a 1930s manor house that had a septic tank leaking fragrant aromas into the house. His wife had mentioned it to Karen Pulte in passing.

That's all Bill needed to hear.

The executive came back from his business trip the following week. The snow was still deep.

He recalled the office conversation: "Bill says, 'Hey, how's it going?' I said, 'Well, we've had people over and they can't find the leak.' He says, 'All right let's get the car. Let's go right now.'

"And we're out there with a flashlight and walking through the woods, walking through the snow. His pants are soaked. Mine are soaked. I wouldn't do this stuff myself, and it's my house. But, Bill's down on his hands and knees trying to find where the blockage is. He's looking for this dye the guys put in the septic to spot the leak.

"I can't imagine any leaders of major organizations who would do something like that," says the executive. "That's a heart of gold. He's a man who truly cares.

"That's his whole life."

The Colonia San Juan, in Guatamala City, was created through the philanthropy of the Quiet Giver. Many families, who once lived on garbage dumps, now call this colorful neighborhood home.

"I'll tell you something," says Fr. Vettese. "I pray for the company all the time. The better they do, the more good I can do. And the more good Bill can do."

"Bill could be living a life of self-indulgence," Fr. Vettese suggests, "but he chooses a simple life. That is really a tremendous example of how to live as a rich man. There's truly evidence that Bill does enter the kingdom of heaven on earth through the goodness he does."

Someday, through his legacy of quiet giving, Bill Pulte's private foundation could rival that of the most generous in the nation. Few, however, will know. The 'how much' will never matter to Bill, nor ever be told. The 'who' will. It will be evident in the faces and hearts of each person saved from drowning in a pool of poverty.

To Bill, his silent acts will only mean that each person who benefits from his generosity might shed the same tears of joy his mother shed years ago, when dawn broke on that quiet morning, and he surprised her with the gift of her dreams.

"Don't worry about what you can get out of something. Be more worried about what you can give."

Chapter Eight
The Visionary

H*ope, imagination, people.*

They fit neatly into a mosaic of Bill Pulte's vision. They are how this company *"got to where it is."*

What Bill has accomplished, what he envisions, is clear and vibrant yet at times roiling and changing beyond the ordinary. His is a vision of *light … color … motion*.

In truth, the last chapter of Bill's story can't be written, may never be. Why? Because what he has accomplished, what he has built from boyhood over several generations, contains momentum.

Bill's vision for Pulte Homes, for the industry, for the house itself, for the world *as we can affect it*, knows no limit, no end. Even beyond the horizon we see, Bill's light shines farther.

What distinguishes Bill as a visionary leader is that he is driven by purpose, not ambition. He achieves, but values determine his decisions. Unchecked ambition without clear values can lead to deceit – or worse.

To see what might be, what's possible, is one of God's gifts to Bill. He receives that gift, murmurs thanks – *he loves what he's doing* – and feels responsible to shape the world because of that blessing. This could be whether he's planning communities, building better homes, finding solutions to poverty … or encouraging any of us to fulfill our dreams.

When we think of people the world admires, whatever our spiritual or political inclinations, the commonality is that each of these beings have a sense of *purpose*. Their lives are dedicated to an ideal, as it relates to their own humanity, and to a more complete world.

Bill Pulte is such a person. His legacy is undeniable. His beacon of light will always shine for others to follow.

"Some of you might be thinking that you can't really make an impact. But, let me remind you how important you are. I believe if each of us works to be the best we can be, we can have a tremendous effect on history."

You know a man by his golf ball.

A Slice, A Vision ... Bill's Beloved Retriever

No, this isn't the story of Bill's hunting dog. He doesn't have one. But like the best Pulte stories, it returns to the heart of a boy with a dream. And it is golden.

"One year, we went to Pebble Beach, in California," says a senior Pulte executive. "It was the mid-1990s. We were playing a golf course called Poppy Hills. It's not a cheap course. Bill and I were in the last group. I was driving the cart.

"Now, the fifth hole is a long Par 5, and it has water right before you get to the green. The pond sits between the fifth and seventh holes.

"On Bill's second shot, he sliced the ball into the water.

"'Can you drive me down there?' Bill asked.

"When we got to the edge of the pond, it was crystal clear. You could easily see 40, 50 golf balls.

"Bill got out of the cart, yanked out his retriever, scooped out his ball. And then another ball. And he waved me up: 'Just go hit your shot.' So I hit my shot and I turned around. He's still pulling balls out. He's probably got a dozen.

"Behind us, there's another group coming up. So Bill waves me up: 'Go ahead and putt out.' We're done. Bill's still pulling balls out of the pond, and by his feet, I can see he's got a good pile – around 15 to 20 golf balls.

"He's not stopping.

"Now, like I said, it's expensive to play this golf course and these balls can't be worth more than 50 cents each. He's already missed the fifth hole and he's still by the pond. The front of his shirt tail is full of balls and he's walking to the other side of the pond, and he lays them out. And he starts digging balls from the other side of the pond.

"So I pull up, and he's got about three dozen. And he gets into the cart and it's like *a kid at Christmas*. He leans close to the compartment in the front of the cart and dumps those golf balls – bump, bump, bump, bump – and you hear them all banging around.

"He's just *beaming*.

"I said, 'You're going to miss $40 worth of golf by my count – and I'm a finance guy – for $20, tops, worth of water-logged golf balls?'

"He stopped what he was doing – looked right at me, and said:

"'*You don't get it.*'

"'When I was a kid, World War II was going on. And my Dad operated a nine-hole municipal golf course. The production of rubber and everything else was dedicated to the war effort, so my Dad couldn't get golf balls to sell in his pro shop.

"'Every night, he would have me and my brother go through the swamps of the course, in our bare feet, mosquitoes everywhere, looking for golf balls. You would feel for the balls with your feet because they'd sink down in the mud. And you would smell when you came out. *It was awful!*

"'I had a recurring dream when I was that age that I would come upon a clear pond just *full* of golf balls.

"'*That* was my dream.'"

For Bill, a vision may take 50 years to achieve. But when it comes true, it is indescribably lucid … even at the end of a 10-foot pole.

Bill and friends playing in a Pro-Am with PGA professional, Fred Funk (middle).

Change, Adapt, Grow

Bill's day-to-day routine at times seems ordinary, but his imagination and vision are not. Nor is our vision, as he invites us to align ours with his.

It has been said that of tomorrow we know nothing, except that Providence will get up for us earlier than the sun. Bill meets Providence on those terms – not knowing what tomorrow brings, but making his first daily act one of thanksgiving. And then, invigorated, he's off to his "giant erector set, his fabulous business," as one executive calls it, where he plans, tinkers, thinks, and fulfills happiness.

In some ways, Bill is childlike: *He has never lost his wonder*. Like a child, his vision is simple. He sees how each person plays a role in that vision. Yet, his vision is wise, knowing, secure, and anchored in a half century of "getting to where it is," through deliberate living and respite with his family. His thinking has been accelerated by decades of decision-making.

"When I started," he says, "if I wanted to make a change to a house, or a strategy, I would go home and think about it for a week, maybe a month. "Now, I look at something and it takes me 30 seconds. That doesn't mean I'm smarter, no. I just can make my mind up quicker. I have gone through that thought process so many times and have seen the end result that I know the answer … *as soon as I see it.*"

Bill has many answers, but readily turns to others when he doesn't, and that keeps him moving.

"My Dad looks to the future," says one of Bill's daughters. "He doesn't wallow in the past. He would always say, don't worry about what happened … He truly is a visionary." Bill has never become enamored with what he has achieved.

"Did you ever figure it?" a Pulte employee asked Bill once. "Did you ever figure the company would become this successful?" "Not in my wildest dreams," Bill answered. "I only hoped to make a few thousand dollars.

"I remember I was in business for five years before I got a $50,000 line of credit and I was on Cloud Nine. Today, I have a billion-dollar line of credit. And you know, I don't even think about it."

Success is immaterial to Bill. His personal wealth has value to him only in this mathematical equation: How many more people can he wrench from poverty?

"That's Bill," says another executive. "The core of this company was created around a man with a dream, and the energy of more committed people than I've ever seen, in all my life."

For the company he chairs, Bill's mantra is change, adapt, grow. Change brings fresh thinking, learning … and winning. A slice of Bill's personal history, as always, provides perspective on this element of Pulte Homes' future. Typical of many Pulte stories, it is set at home.

It was a snowy weekend in the Detroit suburbs, and the young, cooped-up builder decided it wasn't right that four of his children should share the same bathroom, even if it was oversized.

"It was a snowstorm," Bill emphasizes. "That weekend, I changed that bathroom myself. I ended up dividing it into two separate baths – one for the boys, one for the girls.

"It was an ideal time," he says. "I was stuck in my house. I thought: 'I'm going to change it all.'"

He's going to change it all.

He doesn't hesitate. Doesn't think of what he needs or doesn't have. He just does it. It's a simple story, but illustrates he's always been a man of action. He's contemplative only *in* action.

And he's telling us: Be restless, too. Constantly examine why we do what we do, how we do it, when we do it, and how we approach each other, how we build homes and neighborhoods.

And to remember, that despite our restlessness for the future, we need roots, too. "The roots of this company will always be Bill," says a Pulte executive. "We've got to keep those roots firmly planted."

"I was born in the Depression … a time when work was a very valuable thing."

The Glue Of Housing's Future

"When people see Bill, they see a man who started out as a tradesman, pounding the nails, doing the stuff," says a Pulte executive. Bill's long view, his vision of housing's future, comes from the seat of his pants, and his study of housing's evolution. "More and more people want to own their own homes," he says. "It's one of the best investments they can make. The home building business is not going to go away." Big builders are going to get bigger and better, he says, and inefficient builders are "going to go away." High quality, small-town tradesmen will always have a niche, however.

"For a big company that really knows what it's doing, the opportunities are unbelievable," Bill says. And that is only because they have the people, resources, and know-how. By identifying underserved customers, for example, Pulte can focus on markets where demand exceeds supply, homes command premiums, and sales are at a faster pace.

Meanwhile, those homes will be built with materials requiring less maintenance, from vinyl cladding and siding to synthetic trim boards and stone. Inside, homes will be built with more factory-made components, because of the shortage and quality of available labor. That's an issue that goes right to Bill's heart.

"I'll tell you what happened to the tradesmen," he says. "They were proud of their trade or skill, but they wanted to make sure that their sons never got in. That's the big problem: They wanted to make sure their kids went to college. They didn't want them to be out there every day, working in the weather."

Consequently, we'll have more assemblers of fabricated parts, who don't have to know how to use a carpenter's square or power tools, Bill says. "And they hardly ever have to saw anything, if it assembles right."

Bill sees the possible demise of the tradesmen. "I was born in the Depression and work was a very valuable thing," he says. "These days, play is more valuable to many people than work."

So, because of the lack of tradesmen, he sees more innovation to solve the labor gap, and he sees home builders learning from other industries. "If you go into some industries, like the airplane industry, the airplanes are all glued," he says. "So over time, we could end up doing a lot less nailing and more gluing. You won't have to fill the nail hole. Gluing is usually stronger because it's continuous.

"More and more people want to own their own homes. It's one of the best investments they can make."

"The airlines, the way they build planes today, they glue half the skin on the airplanes … it'll outlast any riveted hole. Something you can't believe is how powerful and strong these glues are, compared to nailing and screwing."

Innovations won't be the only things that come from outside housing, as Bill sees it. People will, too. Just look at Pulte's recent hires – they are engineers, lawyers, accountants, marketing experts, and former military officers.

Pulte has to look outside because "the homebuilding industry has been an antiquated business," he says. "It hasn't moved forward like other industries. It's becoming more sophisticated. I mean with a $14 billion organization, you can't do it the same way a guy with a tool belt around his waist is doing it."

Success in this business will always hinge on understanding what the customer wants, says Bill. "There's so many people," he says. "There's so many builders who have no idea what the customer wants.

They know what their spouse wants or what they think is nice. That's what they build into a house. Little builders do that all the time."

That will never be a problem for Pulte, because Bill has seen it all before. He has helped groom the Pulte difference.

The Future Of Pulte Homes

"Homebuilding is one of the best businesses in America," Bill says. "Owning your own home is part of the American Dream."

Pulte Homes has become the go-to builder with a home for every budget. Pulte follows homeowners through every stage in their lives. With 11 segments differentiating families with small children, who need a yard, from retirees who want an extra garage bay for their golf cart, Pulte is building products in every price range.

Bill sees the day when Pulte Homes is the absolute best company to work for in America, setting the world standard for customer delight, getting more than half of its business from referrals, and selling homeowners five homes over their lifetimes.

Bill knows that because Pulte's J.D. Power rankings are at the top in almost every city where the company does business, and because its market share in each segment is becoming more dominant, its achievements in the decades ahead will only be greater. Pulte homes are not only built in half the time they were 30 to 40 years ago, but also with a level of quality other builders find impossible to replicate.

To soar even higher, Pulte will play in different sandboxes: Improving the selection and development of people, fine-tuning consumer segmentation, and achieving operational excellence in design, construction, costing and purchasing, customer relations, and technology.

Not to mention simplification.

"We've lost the simplicity that had to be there when you did everything by hand," says an executive. "And simplicity leads to lower cost; not to lower customer satisfaction or customer delight. But in some ways, we have made things more difficult, for our trade base, and ourselves, through technology.

"In the long run, Bill's completing the loop. To say, OK we've taken the company to here. But how are we going to do 60,000 … 80,000 … 100,000 homes if it's not simple?"

Public Legacy, Personal Love

How does Bill want to be remembered?

"That I built a wonderful company to work for," he says, "that became successful because of its values."

"Bill's goal," says an executive, is "everybody gets to share in what makes Pulte Homes the company it is. He *always* loved what he was doing. He *always* had a vision. He *always* wanted to improve what he was doing. And when he saw his employees get excited about going forward, he'd get more excited."

"What I'm really doing is using my 55 years of business experience to help them save time," Bill says. "I never look back at the past except to have it help me make better decisions or to have the team make better decisions going forward."

Bill Pulte, the architect of a company, admires Thomas Jefferson, the architect of a nation. In his later years, Jefferson wrote: "Though an old man, I am but a young gardener." Bill's garden, too, has been planted, and as a young gardener, he loves watching it grow.

Like Jefferson, Bill will tinker with homes and ideas and notions of how things could be. "I love to remodel houses," Bill admits. "I don't do much of it, but I give people conceptual ideas."

Over dinner with a friend, recently, he sketched plans for a remodel of a lakeside cottage. He drew on a napkin. His friend saved the napkin as a keepsake.

Bill's best ideas somehow always begin on a napkin.

"What I have learned through history, I want to use to make better decisions going forward."

> *"To maintain a joyful family... Each member of the family has to become, in a special way, the servant of the others."*
>
> – Pope John Paul II

Purpose Of Heart

Bill believes all he has, and is, comes from God. His vision, and purpose incorporates all that's possible, because he believes all *is* possible. This goes back to his childhood when his parents couldn't afford the 9 cents it took for him, his brother, and sister to ride the bus to school. Only warm weather and sunshine made the two-mile trip easier. Sunshine meant Bill could ride his bike. To a child, what's more perfect than sunshine, the wind in your hair, and the lightness of being that momentum brings?

Bill is a visionary who carries no cash, who knows a gas tank on "E" still holds a couple of gallons, who has left his empty wallet with airport parking attendants so many times for collateral that the attendants know his family snapshots better than he does.

Why does Bill do these things? Absentmindedness? Depression-era frugality? Or do those habits veil something deeper? Does Bill understand that even with nothing, we can achieve anything? That there's nothing to fear?

One recent Christmas, Bill gave each of his children a bronze sculpture of Christ, a reproduction modeled after one of *Dismas,* the "good thief" who died with Christ and was offered redemption in his final hour.

One of Bill's sons remembers his father's dogged pursuit down the alleyways and backstreets by the Vatican in Rome, looking for the sculptor of the *Dismas* piece, which Bill had purchased with his late wife, Joan, in Italy at least 30 years earlier.

Bill always marveled at the bronze because he was moved by the thief's face and expression, captured by the artist years ago. Bill's wife, Karen, and his daughter-in-law, who speaks basic Italian, rushed with Bill and his son from art shop to art shop, hopping in and out of taxis from Piazza Navona to the Villa Borghese to St. Peter's Square, on the trip's final day.

Bill's daughter-in-law translated Bill's insistent request to shopkeepers in an effort to unravel the mystery of the sculptor. They finally arrived at the right gallery a minute before it closed, their hearts thumping from a wild taxi ride.

"We were searching for a dead man and didn't know it," says Bill's son. At DomusDei Sud, someone told them the artist had, indeed, died, however a sculptor could reproduce crucifixes in the style of the *Dismas* piece. Bill was overjoyed. His Christmas plan for his family was complete.

"To maintain a joyful family requires much from both the parents and the children," Pope John Paul II said. "Each member of the family has to become, in a special way, the servant of the others."

Bill knows how to be that servant, to his family, and to others. Even the most ordinary aspects of our lives can be extraordinary if our sentiments, bonds, and convictions last.

Bill believes in bonds. His convictions are true. He believes any encounter with God restores us to ourselves. And through every encounter with each other, we discover our humanity.

He knows that each of us, in every graced moment, can accomplish what we seek, no matter how empty – or full – our tanks, our pockets … or our hearts.

"People say, 'you're so successful.' I think the poorest guy in the world can be extremely successful under my definition because if he's got inner peace, that's really success. It's got to be there on the inside."

Every Day A Miracle

Bill arises each day as if it had a miracle stuffed inside it, and for him, it still does. He's doing what he loves, something he discovered on his storied journey through life. His work became his passion over years of breathing the unmistakable aroma of cut lumber.

But, his purpose grew over years of working amidst the back-and-forth camaraderie of co-workers, on the job site, or in the board room. He never knew what tomorrow would bring, except that *Providence would get up for him earlier than the sun*.

"People say, when are you going to take off and play golf?" Bill says. "Well even when I was playing good, I would rather go to work and build houses or design lots. It isn't stress because it's fun." Bill will never leave Pulte Homes. "He will stay until he is not able to contribute," says an executive. "He wants to always be a part of this."

Says another executive: "Bill told me, 'You know, every home builder, after the founder and namesake was no longer involved, went by the wayside. It didn't survive. *And this company is going to survive.*' In his heart of hearts, he knows Pulte Homes will be Pulte Homes for forever."

What drives Bill today are endless possibilities. As chairman, he guides the selection of leaders and he helps those leaders develop new leaders. It's part of his plan. *He always has a plan.*

"Pulte Homes' beginning was *the man*, but it was the man knowing how to get the right people and to build … and to build and build," says an executive. "Not just homes, but to build on all the right things that made Pulte, and put Bill Pulte where he is today."

If Pulte's story doesn't end, where does it go? How does it get there?

For that, just glance at the past, for an instant, then lock in on the beacon scanning ahead. Bill's guiding light transcends the horizon. And while we look ahead, he reminds us, too, to peer within.

> *"I'd say Pulte Homes is as successful as it is today not because of Bill Pulte, but because of all the wonderful people who work here."*

We'll think of him ending his day, as he ends most days – flicking off his office light. Heading to his Cadillac, the car he pined for in 1948 as he labored in 98-degree heat atop an asphalt roof, the shingles scorching the soles of his boots. Bill will grab his keys, on his car's front mat, like always.

The engine will kick to life, and with the passion for what he does still burning within him, his purpose still driving him, he will move forward, just as he did on his first day in business – *our* business – the future bright, and ever, always, *ahead*.

He'll always be our visionary, our family man, whose entrepreneurialism and whiz-kid inspirations help us find new ways to be competitors. His example of quiet giving makes us strong, happy, and humble, ready to lead and teach the Pulte Way.

You are a wonderful light – Bill Pulte.
We will follow.
We will lead.

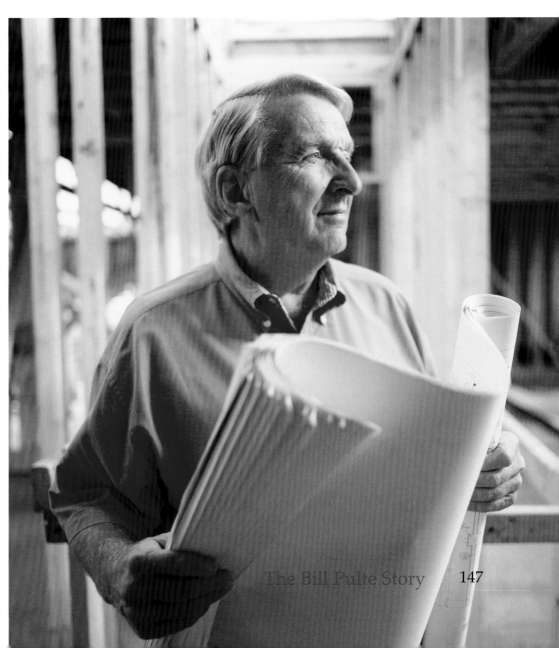

The Bill Pulte Story   147